Understanding Representation

Understanding Representation

Jen Webb

Los Angeles • London • New Delhi • Singapore • Washington DC

© Jen Webb 2009

First published 2009

Apart from any fair dealing for the purposes of research or
private study, or criticism or review, as permitted under the
Copyright, Designs and Patents Act, 1988, this publication
may be reproduced, stored or transmitted in any form, or by
any means, only with the prior permission in writing of the
publishers, or in the case of reprographic reproduction, in
accordance with the terms of licences issued by the Copyright
Licensing Agency. Enquiries concerning reproduction outside
those terms should be sent to the publishers.

SAGE Publications Ltd
1 Oliver's Yard
55 City Road
London EC1Y 1SP

SAGE Publications Inc.
2455 Teller Road
Thousand Oaks, California 91320

SAGE Publications India Pvt Ltd
B 1/I 1 Mohan Cooperative Industrial Area
Mathura Road
New Delhi 110 044

SAGE Publications Asia-Pacific Pte Ltd
33 Pekin Street #02-01
Far East Square
Singapore 048763

Library of Congress Control Number: 2007933814

British Library Cataloguing in Publication data

A catalogue record for this book is available from
the British Library

ISBN 978-1-4129-1918-0
ISBN 978-1-4129-1919-7 (pbk)

Typeset by C&M Digitals (P) Ltd, Chennai, India
Printed in India at Replika Press Pvt Ltd
Printed on paper from sustainable resources

Contents

Acknowledgements

The author and publishers would like to thank the following for permission to use:

Figures 0.1, 1.2, 1.3, 2.7, 3.4, 3.5 © Paul Travers 2006

Figure 3.1 and 3.2 © James Webb 2005

Page 14 T.S. Eliot, excerpt from 'East Coker' in *Four Quartets* © 1940 by T.S. Eliot and renewed in 1968 by Esme Valerie Eliot, reprinted by permission of Harcourt, Inc.

Page 27 Margaret Atwood, excerpt from 'This is a photograph of me', permission granted by House of Anansi Press.

Page 39 W.S. Graham, excerpt from 'What is the language using us for?', permission granted by Michael and Margaret Snow.

Page 42 EE Cummings, excerpt from 'r-p-o-p-h-e-s-s-a-g-r' © 1935, © 1963, 1991 by the Trustees for the E.E. Cummings Trust. © 1978 by George James Firmage, from Complete Poems: 1904–1962 by E.E. Cummings, edited by George J. Firmage. Used by permission of Liveright Publishing Corporation.

Page 44 Walter Abish, *Alphabetical Africa* © 1974. Reprinted by permission of New Directions Publishing Corp.

Page 68 Michael and Corinne White, for permission to use images at Figure 3.3

Page 73 Primo Levi, *A Tranquil Star*, reproduced by permission of Penguin Books Ltd. Translated by Ann Goldstein and Alessandra Bastagli © 2007 by Goldstein and Alessandra Bastagli. Used by permission of W.W. Norton and Company, Inc.

Page 91 Thanks to Eddie Izzard for permission to reproduce material from *Dress to Kill* (1998).

Pages 124 and 125 Thanks to Chaco Kato to reproduce 'In a rainy room' and 'Migration'.

Page 130 J M Coetzee, *The Life and Times of Michael K*, published by Secker & Warburg, reprinted by permission of the Random House Group Ltd. © J.M. Coetzee, 1983. All rights reserved. Used by permission of the Peter Lampack Agency Inc.

Introduction: The terms of representation

'Representation' is a remarkably common term. It is used in many different fields, professions and domains; it pops up on the news; it even makes an appearance in everyday conversations. It should, therefore, be a very familiar term, easily understood by anyone. A quick examination of any dictionary, or of the super-dictionary that is the internet, will provide a number of definitions of representation. Some are philosophical in scope: for instance, explanations of what Kant wrote about representation. Some are more or less linguistic: discussions of how meanings are made through the production and organization of **signs**. Others are ethnographic, or anthropological: analyses of how people from other cultures make meanings and ascribe values. Because the term is used in psychology and philosophy, film and literary studies, media and communication, art and visual culture, politics and government, sociology and linguistics, it has many different nuances and uses.

In most of these disciplines, though, representation is examined as a way of teasing out the embedded, underlying meanings of texts. How women are represented in a film, for instance, can be seen to convey both the attitude of the film maker to women, and the general way women are viewed, understood, or 'known' in a particular context – the context in which the film was made and distributed. How someone represents their personal history or their feelings gives insights into their psychological wellbeing, or how they make sense of the world – how their brains function, and how they understand themselves and their environments. In political and legal contexts, the word describes the process by which an agent stands in for – represents – a constituency or a client. It is used by linguists to explain how a sound can stand in for an object or concept. It is used by social scientists to determine how closely the characteristics of a group of people match the characteristics of the population as a whole, and thus how widely the findings of a research project can be applied.

Representation is also fundamental to everyday life. People practice representation all the time because we live immersed in representation: it is how we understand our environments and each other. It is also how we both *are*, and how we understand ourselves; representation is implicated in the process of *me* becoming *me*. None of us is like Popeye (*I yam what I yam*); rather, each of us is produced through a complex mix of background, tastes, concerns, training, tendencies, experiences – all made real to us through the principles and processes of representation that frame and govern our experiences of being in the world. The frames thus generated do not give us a stable or permanent sense of being in the world, but one that is frequently confusing, and always subject to change – as this image suggests. What we see is not what is there, but what our social and cultural traditions and their contexts give us.

Figure 0.1 © Paul Travers 2006

Central to all its uses, and domains of use, are three questions: who is performing the representation; what does it mean; and what effects does it have? This is also the approach taken in this book: in the chapters that follow I will trace how the term is used in meaning-making, language, politics and society, art and the media, to suggest useful approaches not only to research, but also to understanding how we personally experience the nature of the world and of being.

REPRESENTATION AND REALITY

A central issue in representation is that of substitution: it is widely understood as the process of standing in for someone or something, or acting as a substitute for the 'real thing'. A female character in a movie is seen to *stand in for* women everywhere; the words someone uses to tell their story *stand in for* the neurological processes that structure communication; the thirty people who participate in a social research study *stand in for* the population more generally. This is a perfectly reasonable approach: after all, we know that there are concrete things in the world, and there are ways of describing or portraying those things. There is a difference between ideas about a thing, and the thing itself – as expressed in a famous line of poetry by Wallace Stevens. There are differences between actuality and imagination, or report and story. Aren't there? Let's test it out by a simple experiment:

> You are looking at this page. It is covered with black squiggles that you recognize as alphabetical notations that, brought into combinations, form words, phrases, sentences and paragraphs. As you look, you decode these squiggles and turn them into sounds in your head or maybe read them out loud. What you 'hear' in your head, or actually hear if you read them out loud, are sounds that represent the squiggles. Those squiggles themselves both represent ideas in my head, and commonly accepted ways of communicating in written form. There is nothing in these sets of squiggles that has any direct material connection to any material thing. I say 'head' but no head appears – only the idea of it. I say 'page', but it is only four individual squiggles: P-A-G-E. Together these form what any English speaker trained to read alphabetical script will recognize as a word for something that might or might not be present. It is an abstraction; it is not the page itself.
>
> Now let's make it more concrete. First, read this paragraph so you have the instructions clear in your head, and then put down the book and go outside. As you go, look at and touch the things you pass: run your fingers along the wall, be aware of the sensation of flooring under your feet, grasp the door handle and be conscious of its shape and texture. Now you are outside. Smell the scents on the air, and identify them (exhaust fumes, the perfume of plants, garbage not yet collected by the authorities). Feel on your skin the movement of a breeze, perhaps, or the touch of rain, or the heat of the sun. Look around you: you might see sky, trees, road, buildings – real things in your immediate ambit. And you should be able to hear sounds too: a dog barking, traffic in a nearby street, perhaps the ringing of a telephone. These are real things: they are objects and sensations that have a material presence. They are real things that touch your skin, or are processed by your auditory, olfactory and optical nerves. You are physically outside your house, and also outside the abstract world of books and writing; you are immersed in a sea of sensory presence.
>
> Now go back inside, and pick up this book again.

Compare your experiences with the descriptions of those experiences, above. How real are the descriptions, compared with your experience of the 'real' world? Probably, the words were considerably less 'real', present and physical than your few minutes outside the house. Squiggles on a page cannot compare with the actuality, the physicality, of things that touch your body and are registered by your senses rather than by the technologies of speech and reading you have learned.

BEYOND REPRESENTATION?

Does this mean that your experience is outside the domain of representation – that it cannot be sufficiently described, but can only be felt in a way that is beyond language? This is a contentious point for many scholars in the field. Christopher Prendergast, for instance, insists that 'Everything is representable' (2000: 1), and many theorists, especially in the later part of the twentieth century, agree that humans have no real access to the world itself; our understanding and experience of the world can only be second hand, mediated through systems of representation. But others disagree, and point out that there are things that are beyond representation: or, at least, beyond satisfactory articulation. No one can actually understand or represent their own death, for instance, because the moment of the experience renders you incapable of understanding, communicating or representing what is going on, or how you feel (in fact, of course, you no longer feel!).

There are other examples sometimes called 'unrepresentable' – commentators speaking of the Holocaust, for instance, have insisted that its horror is so vast that it cannot be reduced and contained by representation. This is the position taken by the critic Theodor Adorno who insisted that 'To write poetry after Auschwitz is barbaric' (981: 34). This does not mean that it is in fact incapable of being represented, but that Adorno considers it inappropriate to attempt to capture its appalling scope in the limited space of representation. Others find the idea of God beyond representation, so much so that the divine name cannot be spoken or written. This seems to rest on a combination of the incapacity of human language to capture the divine, and the lack of respect that would be implied by simply chatting about God. There are other objects considered unrepresentable because to represent them would be to go against God's instructions – the iconoclastic aspects of Judaism or Islam, for instance, which forbid portraits and other 'lifelike' representations.

But of course these examples do not forcefully undermine the notion that representation governs our experience of the world. Although we cannot effectively represent death, as I pointed out above, we know it exists, through the limited (and often flawed) representations of the world that we make and perceive. As Prendergast writes, what these examples point out is either that the terms of representation are inadequate, or that representation is forbidden:

'It is not that representation as such is impossible; it is rather that it fails in its task' (2000: 2). In the art world, for instance, there are many things that are 'beyond representation' that are nonetheless captured in non-representational art. In some such cases, it may not be that the event or object is really incapable of being represented, but that the artist has refused the logic of representation, and is attempting instead to convey a 'something else' – a mood, a feeling. Samuel Beckett's novels and short stories are well-known examples of this. He typically eschews plot and structure for what is called 'affect' – a feeling, an attitude or emotion. His characters are in no identifiable place, wrestling with unknown problems or being assaulted for no obvious reason by unknown agents. They worry, and wonder, and fret, but do not achieve resolution. In his theatre piece *Play* (1964) the characters speak neither to each other nor to the audience; they simply direct their voices out into nothingness. Nor does the plot actually go anywhere: the characters simply run through the arcane script a couple of times, making no connection with each other – often speaking over each other so that the audience can't tell what is being said – and then their voices peter out, the lights go down, and the play is over.

This is not an example of something truly unrepresentable; it is an example of an artist making the choice to be non-representational because that choice allows him to suggest people's incapacity to connect with one another, and their inability to make sense of or stick to the 'script' of life. Of course it does so (ironically) in the material of representation: using words, gestures, utterances, clothing, and set and lighting design. In its very non-representationality, it shows that it is not possible to speak of representation without representing – we are caught in a logical and practical loop.

THE LIMITS OF EXPERIENCE

One strand of this loop is the fact that there is little actual difference between the experience of physical stimuli, and the mental abstraction of reading and thought. This might seem unlikely; but as I will discuss in the following chapters, the gap between the 'real world' and 'mere representation' is not always as evident as common-sense would suggest. New research into how the brain works is shifting our understanding of how individuals make sense of the world, and convey sense to others. Neuroscientists, social scientists and philosophers argue that rather than representation being a straightforward matter of signs standing in for, and communicating, real things, it is an **episte-mological** process. In other words, representation is considerably more than a simple matter of standing in for; it is also productive of what we know, and how we know it: that is to say, it is constitutive – it makes us. As well, those scholars argue, representation is **ontological**: that is, it is about the nature of being; it is tied up with what something actually is, of what it is constituted, its status as a thing, property, object or experience. They also define representation as **cognitive**, an aspect of brain function, because much of the work of representation happens below the level of consciousness. When you stepped outside a few minutes ago to experience the 'real world' beyond the pages of a book, what you experienced might have felt real, but in fact was just bits of data that your brain processed and returned to you as sensations. Finally, they argue, representation is **axiological**. This means that it involves questions of ethics, or the 'right' way of seeing, knowing and doing. Representation is, in short, how we experience and communicate ourselves and the world we inhabit, how we know ourselves, and how we deal with others.

This is not to suggest that real, concrete objects do not exist in their own right, independent of representation. After all, the body and the world have physical properties that are not mediated by language or culture. If I stub my toe, the world has made itself present to me; and I both experience and interpret that moment, as that old limerick reminds us:

There was a faith healer from Deal
Who said, although pain isn't real
When I sit on a pin
And it punctures my skin
I dislike what I fancy I feel.

The faith healer can only retain belief in the absence of actuality by reframing experience. This is not a useful way to understand the relationship between representation and reality because it distorts commonly shared understandings, or codes, about the world and its meanings, and thus makes it difficult to communicate, or to be taken seriously by others.

Sometimes this is a good thing: common understandings and codes are not necessarily useful or 'true' in the sense of having a close connection with the observed world. Think of how throughout the eighteenth and nineteenth centuries it was possible for Europeans to understand – to encode – African people as 'not really human'. It was a 'wrong' representation, but still a profoundly effective one (at least, from the European perspective – African people would have had very different understandings of their own identity) because it allowed slave traders, ships' captains, governments, slave owners and the whole social realm to treat black people as commodities, not as human beings. Those who rejected this representation fell out of communication: Africans were traded like goods, and Europeans who challenged that representation (and the practice of slavery) were ignored, repulsed or prosecuted. Eventually however the terms of representation and hence the treatment of people shifted: slavery was outlawed, and though racism remains firmly entrenched, the official representation of Africans is as human beings. Contemporary acts of slavery are abhorred and where feasible are prosecuted, and the view of the world is radically different from its earlier iteration: the 'truth' of slavery, and of the relative identity of European and African peoples, has changed.

It is important always to bear in mind that the 'truth' of any representation is always only true insofar as it is perceived and coded as such by people. What seems to be true, right or accurate is, generally speaking, only true, right or accurate when it fits with a particular social, historical and personal perspective. To see 'things as they are' in fact means only to see 'things as I/my culture frame them', or 'things as I/my culture want them to be'. Any representation is limited, flawed and interested; and any representation changes 'things as they are' if it makes those things present in a different way.

THE LIMITS OF THE LEXICON

Some of the complexities of the concept of representation – what it can mean, where it can mean, the limits on its meaning – come about because representation is a slippery term, particularly in English. The German language allows more carefully delineated senses of the word: *Darstellung* (making present), *Vertretung* (speaking for and standing in for), *Wortvorstellung* (representations of words), and *Sach-* or *Dingvorstellung* (representations of things) allow fairly precise uses of the term. But in English we have just one word for all these forms and modes – and, indeed, even to talk about representation itself. This entire book, for instance, is a representation of representation. This raises a further problem because unless we have a very clear understanding of what the word means, or what I mean by it in the previous clause, it is very difficult to get any practical sense out of it. The limits of the English language mean that we are using just one word to do multiple duties, and to mean a variety of things. But because it is the same word in each instance of use, we tend to behave as though there is a commonality among all its meanings. Jacques Derrida takes up this point:

> If the noun 'representation', the adjectives 'representing,' 'representable,' 'representative', the verbs 'represent' or 'represent oneself' are not only the grammatical modulations of a single and identical meaning, if kernels of different meanings are present, at work in or produced by these grammatical modes of the idiom, then the lexicologist, the semanticist, indeed the philosopher who would try to classify different varieties of 'representation' or of 'representing' ... is going to have a rough time of it. (1982: 299)

As he goes on to argue, the words do not have a 'single and identical meaning', which is the main reason, perhaps, for the complexity of the concept, and the many squabbles among scholars about just what the term means, and what effects it has. We 'have a rough time of it' because it is not possible to settle on just what it means. Having said that, I will attempt to settle on some meanings, and to provide some definitions – always remembering that their 'truth' is limited and contingent.

DEFINITIONS OF REPRESENTATION

Christopher Prendergast suggests some definitions for the term 'representation'. The first, he writes, 'is the sense of represent as re-present, to make present again, in two interrelated ways, spatial and temporal' (2000: 4). It cites, or 'quotes', a presence, referring to something that is not there, but is assumed to be authentic and potentially present (the authentic voice, and so on). This is representation as *Darstellung*, the notion of making or *rendering* presence. In this mode, a particular representation can have the capacity to make visible, in the here and now, something that was (or might have been) present in a different here and now – it accommodates both space (it *is* present) and time (it *is in* the present).

The second sense Prendergast offers is that of *delegating* presence, or *Vertretung*: the substitution of something for something or someone else. This is most commonly seen in language and politics. In language, a word makes a concrete thing, or an idea, present in conversation or writing. I say 'elephant', and though there is no elephant in the room, the concept of elephant is rendered, or brought into consciousness – allowed to stand in for the animal. In politics, a person is nominated to stand in for, speak for and *represent*, me. I delegate my political voice to a substitute in government, in a trade union or in a court of law. In both language and politics, this sense of representation allows a term, image or agent to substitute for an absent object, idea or person.

MAKING IT HAPPEN

So far, so good, and this should be very familiar to anyone with the most basic common-sense understanding of representation. But of course there is a lot more going on in the process. There is, for instance, the issue of origins: the verb 'to make' (*making* meaning, *making* a constituent present in the person of their representative) is important here because representation does not necessarily just happen. Unlike physical events – the sun that rises and sets without anyone's intervention – representation is *made* to happen; and it is made to happen by people. This is representation that performs an action, representation as a verb. It makes present what is absent, and so adds something to the context. And it does this through the actions of people: 'We see representation as a *process* in which the makers of signs, whether adult or child, seek to make a representation of some object or entity', write Gunther Kress and Theo van Leeuwen (1996: 6), and this seeking and making is often direct and conscious. A work of art, or a policy document; an address to the nation, or a seminar presentation; the blueprints for a new bridge, or a tax return – each is a representation which almost certainly is crafted very deliberately and consciously, with the audience very much in mind, to produce an intended result.

This is not the only way to understand it, however. A great many of the representations each of us generate in our everyday lives are not at the level of consciousness, but are simply our habitual ways of speaking, writing or otherwise acting. Think, for instance, of someone at a board meeting who is lounging in her chair, legs sprawled out in front of her, head thrown back, arms loosely crossed across her chest. Now compare her with another person at that imagined board meeting whose back is entirely vertical, whose head is precisely attuned to his spine, whose chair is tucked up under the board table so that it is impossible to see his legs, and so on. Each person is giving a very different impression of their sense of self in relation to that meeting. The first is confident, and probably bored. The second is very formal, more guarded, and is taking the whole process much more seriously. Each is making a representation of self and of the meeting, and conveying this representation to others; it is quite likely that neither has planned, intended or thought through what they are representing, or why. Still, they are making their thoughts manifest and present – representing them – to others around the table.

ESTABLISHING EQUIVALENCE

Much of the work of representation depends on first having established relationships of equivalence. Before we can start naming or substituting for, we must make it possible for 'a' to mean, or substitute for, 'b'. This involves establishing relationships of equivalence between a word or other sign, and the concept and thing that is observed – the **referent**. What is the process by which 'elephant' becomes connected with a large mammal? I won't attempt to answer that – it is a question better directed to lexicographers or linguists – but we need to understand that there is no natural equivalence between signs and referents, only equivalences that come out of particular cultural practices and cultural codes. This is an aspect of the process of delegation.

Once that equivalence is established – so that, say, people equate the word 'elephant' with the mammal – then the work of making it present can be accomplished: 'elephant' (the sign) now renders Elephant (the creature). The word makes the creature present, because the word has come to stand in for the creature through the process of crafting chains of equivalence.

But it doesn't stop there: representation is a complex and slippery process because it is cultural and not natural, therefore not necessary or fixed. The sign itself is always empty of real content. Let's look again at 'elephant'; I can only say that word meaningfully because as a culture we have earlier established those chains of equivalence between the huge mammal and the word. 'Elephant' (the sign) doesn't inevitably mean Elephant (the creature); it is only a series of letters pushed together to make a sound we identify as the thing itself. Because it doesn't necessarily mean the animal, it also doesn't only mean the animal: the word might be used as a substitute for, or to make present, a toy, a rhyming sound, a character in a book, something else that is very large … it is empty except when it is put to work in a specific context, and for people who can decode it.

REPRESENTATION AND CONSTITUTION

In short, the processes of representation do not simply make connections, relationships and identities *visible*: they actually *make* those connections, relationships and identities. Representation is not just about substitution and reiteration, but is about *constitution*: it constitutes – makes real – both the world and our ways of being in the world and in communities.

Let's go back to the basic common-sense way in which representation is put to work: someone does or says something; that something is read by others as being an act of representation that is conveying something; and a further something is likely to occur as a result. This is a very conventional description of representation, especially in discussions about the media: Kate Bowles points out that representation is often considered 'simply the question of how the media portray events, people and ideas, and how that portrayal then influences the real world of events, people and ideas' (2002: 72). What is missing in this depiction is the *systematic* nature of representation: it should be understood not just as a noun – representation as a portrayal, or an object; but also as a verb – representation as the action involved, and the processes that must be gone through, in the work of making words or gestures. Stuart Hall explains that 'the production of the meaning of the concepts in our minds through language' is a system of representation because it refers to clusters of ways of conceptualizing, organizing and arranging signs and concepts, and their relationships (1997a: 17). So representation is not just about rendering and delegating, but is also about organizing and arranging knowledge and ideas.

This is as much a cognitive as a linguistic or political idea. The processes we use to organize and arrange knowledge are cognitive processes because they require that we perceive ideas, or sense data, and connect them to objects 'out there' – concrete objects. And we all do this, all the time: we constantly, if subconsciously, produce meanings out of the material world. Pure silence, or pure unmediated experience, is not a function of living human beings. Pure silence is available only to the dead, who no longer have the capacity to see, hear or feel anything, or to make sense of their environment. Unmediated experience is available perhaps only to non-sentient objects – rocks or motorcars – because anything with a brain is always subject to the chattering of neurons, the brain's constant effort to process and analyse what we are seeing, hearing or feeling.

We have to organize our knowledge and ideas because we do not have direct access to the things 'out there' – the things we are seeing, hearing or feeling – and so cannot directly experience and process them. Writings on cognition suggest that there are always at least two degrees of separation between me and the object I am contemplating: first, I am separated from it because the process of perception translates it from an object to an image in my mind. Next, I am separated again because I translate that image into other signs so that I can represent it, if only to myself. Think again of my mythical elephant: many years ago in Africa I stood in the veld and watched a herd of elephant about two hundred metres from me; I experienced a spatial, but not a temporal, separation from them. But more separations were, necessarily, involved. 'Seeing' meant cutting them out from everything else in my range of vision, using the cones and rods in my eyes to capture the shape and colour of the animals, using my binocular vision to triangulate the scene and thus produce a sense of their size relative to their surroundings, and process all this data to come up with the picture of 'elephant'. Then I had to sift through all the concepts in my memory to find the word 'elephant' and with it all the associations of 'huge', 'dangerous', 'funny', 'like Babar', and so on. This is a long and terribly complicated process handled in the flickering of moments by any normal brain, but it does mean that the elephants themselves, out there in the veld, were doubly separated from me, first by being rendered as image, and then by being displaced by the word 'elephant', their delegate in my thoughts.

My point is that we can be conscious of things around us only insofar as we have ideas about them, the language to name them, and thereby to perceive them closely. We are not thinking them into being – they certainly have their own existence – but we do think ourselves into relationship with them. This notion of representation supports the idea of a mediated world, where our connection with everything outside ourselves is always mediated by perception and representation. Something always stands in for an external thing by means of **resemblance** or symbolism, so our knowledge of that external thing 'is thus indirect, in that it is mediated by the ideas, which are as it were clues to, or evidence for, the external things that act on our senses' (Dickerson 2004: 10).

THE STRUCTURE OF THIS BOOK

This introduction has focused on some of the definitions of representation, and some of the complexities of the concept. It cannot cover them all because the concept is too vast and too messy to be neatly encapsulated in a list, or a book, or a shelf of books. Derrida posits the endless messiness and murkiness of representation in his vision of Socrates stumbling into a symposium, and saying:

> You tell me this is aesthetic, political, metaphysical, historic, religious and episte-mological representation, as if each were one among others, but in the end, aside from the fact that you are perhaps forgetting some types, that you are probably enumerating too many or too few, you have not answered the question: what is representation in itself and in general? What makes all these representations representations called by the same name? What is the eidos of representation, the being-representation of representation? (1982: 302)

This introduction has attempted to stumble towards at least some of the questions, if not the answers, of 'what is representation in itself and in general?'. In the following chapters I trace how representation works in some of Socrates' modes. In Chapter 1 I turn to the historical and epistemological by discussing the relationship between resemblance, reality and representation and how, in the Western tradition, these dominant modes of communication developed and are applied.

In Chapter 2 the issue of language is explored, and the uses of semiotic and discursive analyses of language, communication and meaning-making. There are several, often contesting, schools of thought on how representation works. I will outline the main issues of the reflective, intentional and constructivist 'schools', and describe some of the tools used by theorists to make sense of representative moments or texts. This brings in some of the history of representation: what is often called the 'linguistic turn', when scholars began to focus on using **semiotics** (the science of signs) to analyse texts; and the 'cultural turn', which tends to focus on the techniques of discourse analysis to make sense of social practices and structures. Each offers a very different notion of how meanings are made, and what it means to mean, and I will explore these differences in approach to set out the ways in which communication acts are performed by 'writers' and 'readers', and ways of decoding the world of texts.

Representation is not a purely human characteristic; it is also found in other sentient creatures; but my focus in this book is on people, so in Chapter 3 I look at the human beings who are involved in making and decoding these representations. What does it mean to be a 'speaking subject', a person with ideas, perspectives, and cultural and contextual specificities, who makes use of the tools of communication and understanding that can seem so prescriptive? How do our brains, memories and cultural frameworks shape how we both make and analyse meanings? How do we, individually and as communities or nations, 'automatically' know the categories by which individuals and groups are classified and valued: issues such as class, gender, race, sexuality, ethnicity, age and other markers of difference? What does it mean for all of us, as the subjects of representation – representing subjects – to live in the contemporary arrangements of nations and communities, and contemporary communication networks?

This raises the issue of what are called the agents of communication. **Agency** is a catch-all term that incorporates human communication, knowledge and activity, and it is deployed as a name for any individual or collective that acts in society. Some agents are collectives: social institutions like government departments, education, the religious community and so on, which produce and manage meaning. Other agents are individual people making meaning in their everyday lives and in specific sites (professional and personal). Such individuals, consciously or not, draw on their own culture and its traditions, the shape of the language they speak, the properties of their brains, their sensory capacities and experiences, and the particularities of their own bodies (gender, age, ethnicity and so on) to represent themselves as well as any meanings they wish to make.

Chapter 4 extends this material by looking at how, as human beings, we organize ourselves politically. Politics is the site in which what something might mean is broadly determined. Most theorists agree that meanings are crafted, and are cultural artefacts rather than fragments of the real. But most human beings (including theorists) acknowledge that while 'sticks and stones may break my bones, words will *really* hurt me'. This chapter investigates the social and political dimensions of representation, because it is not (as will be clear from the foregoing paragraphs) just a matter of squiggles or lines. Rather, representation is at the heart of all systems of government, whether democratic, theocratic or aristocratic, because in every instance government is invested in an idea of someone or some group of individuals or institutions standing in for – representing – something: me, my community, god, the divine right of kings, and so on.

The next chapter discusses some of the effects of linguistic, social and political organization in what is called 'cultural representation'. This deals both with what most people understand as 'artistic' or 'cultural' activities – the work of artists and novelists and film makers, the function of museums and galleries – and with less obviously artistic, but still highly cultural, media of representation, such as newspapers and television. The central issue is the significance of context and framing in making cultural representations, and communicating them effectively to others. This incorporates the poetics of representation: how it actually works in terms of the way something is said or shown, and how specific forms of representation such as story, **analogy**, **metaphor**, syntax and spatiality contribute to how meanings are made in particular contexts, and for particular purposes. I also address the relationship between visual and verbal modes, and between written and oral modes of representation, to discuss the craft of meaning-making and how it can be used consciously. This incorporates an understanding of the relationship between showing and telling; and how specific kinds of sign (a word, sound or image that means something) and figure (metaphor, analogy, trope) likewise shape what meanings can be derived from something that is heard or seen.

Finally, in the conclusion of this book, I discuss the politics of representation in the sense of the ethical dimensions of how we delegate, render and organize objects, ideas and meanings. If things are changed when framed or represented differently, then there is an ethical obligation on every person to think through what representations they make, considering how others and how external things might be affected by what they say and do, and by how they perform their lives and relationships.

Decades ago the poet TS Eliot wrote, in 'East Coker', lines that seem directed at the problem of representation:

> So here I am, in the middle way, having had twenty years
> … Trying to use words, and every attempt
> Is a wholly new start, and a different kind of failure
> Because one has only learnt to get the better of words
> For the thing one no longer has to say, or the way in which
> One is no longer disposed to say it. And so each venture
> Is a new beginning, a raid on the inarticulate
> With shabby equipment always deteriorating
> In the general mess of imprecision of feeling,
> Undisciplined squads of emotion. (1969: 182)

Understanding representation requires us to make *raids on the inarticulate*, in an attempt to render it articulate. This is always terribly difficult, because we can only perceive and articulate in a sort of a blur, and with limited perspective. We perceive always in context; often in confusion; and sometimes in what Eliot elsewhere in 'East Coker' called 'the intolerable wrestle/With words and meanings'. Meaning is never clean and clear, and the making of meaning is never done; we mean or understand meaning only for a moment, before the context, the perception, and the meanings shift. This is the context of meaning-making, and of the perception without which meaning cannot take place. However, by learning how to use our 'shabby equipment' and how to use words variously in various contexts, it is possible to sharpen up the blur, to make 'new beginnings' in communicating with one another, and to tidy up, with thought and evidence, 'the general mess of imprecision of feeling'.

1 Resemblance, representation and reality

Communication is central to how we get along in the world: how we make meanings, and how we both make sense of, and organize, our environments. It includes not only spoken and written language, but also visual imagery, bodily gestures, music, architectural design, and all the many other ways by which we insert ourselves into, and communicate with, the world. Representation is the dominant system by which we handle communication, but it is not the only option. In fact, it is a comparatively new system for meaning-making: a number of other conceptual frameworks and systems served for many centuries and, in some cases, continue to serve.

It is only in the past few hundred years – the modern era, the period from about the seventeenth century on – that representation, strictly speaking, has dominated approaches to the use of language and the construction of meaning. As Christopher Prendergast writes:

> as a concept supplying a regulatory matrix of thought, representation, notwithstanding its ancient lineage, is an essentially modern invention, one of the master concepts of modernity underpinning the emergence of what Heidegger called the Age of the World Picture, based on the epistemological subject/object split of the scientific outlook: the knowing subject who observes ('enframes' is Heidegger's term) the world-out-there in order to make it over into an object of representation. (2000: 2)

Of course there have always been gestures towards what we now understand as representation: ways of separating ourselves from the objects and ideas under discussion, systems of delegation, and substitutions. The idols that stand in for gods in ancient cultures are substitionary, and so are representational. But how people have understood themselves in relation to both the world and the systems of communication has changed radically over the centuries. An earlier model, and one that continues to inflect our perception of and organizing of the world, is resemblance.

BEFORE REPRESENTATION

Stuart Hall describes as 'the reflective' approach to language (1997a: 15) the notion that a sign reflects an already-existing meaning or identity. This approach was written about in very ancient texts – those of the Greek philosophers, for instance, where it is named **mimesis**, or resemblance, or similitude. The idea is that the sign actually *resembles*, and does not simply *signify*, the thing itself. Although like representation-proper it stands in for the original thing, it does so in a direct relationship based on imitation, or likeness.

Mimesis, or resemblance, can be found in virtually all human mark-making or other cultural practices. A portrait that looks like its subject; music that sounds like the wind rustling the leaves of a tree; clothes that resemble the feathers of a bright bird; a garden designed to look like a forest – all these are mimetic signs. It can also be a mode of writing, especially in pictographic forms like Egyptian hieroglyphics or Mandarin characters. Here the writing is a series of marks that act as signs because they stand in for the topic under discussion (they 'represent' that topic). But unlike symbolic representation, they communicate by looking like the things to which they refer. The written sign for water, for instance, might be a series of wave-like lines. The written sign for a god might look like statues of that god; and the statues themselves might have elements that resemble the qualities attributed to that god: perhaps huge muscles for power, a lion's head for nobility, a snake's body for speed, and so on.

Ancient Egyptian hieroglyphs are perhaps the best-known of written texts based on resemblance; they use many pictographic elements, along with abstract signs, to tell complex stories, relate dense histories, and to record bureaucratic matters such as policies or budgets. The more famous objects are sarcophagi, and thanks to the efforts of Egyptologists there are many examples of tombs and other iconography and objects of the dead in museums around the world.

The image here (from an exhibition at the British Museum) is inscribed on the tomb of a royal woman from Thebes, who died about 530BCE. I cannot read the hieroglyphs, but I assume – based on other sarcophagi – that the story told on the whole object, of which this is a tiny extract, describes her life and times, and comments on her death. There are recognizable images: an ibis, a scarab, an eye and a person extending an arm; there are other more abstracted icons, such as the jagged and curved lines and other marks that bear no obvious resemblance to anything. I can recognize, or think I recognize, elements in the text; but I can only guess at the meaning of the signs and the text as a whole, based on what I think the inscriptions resemble, and what little I know about ancient Egyptian culture.

Figure 1.1   Inscription on an Egyptian tomb, British Museum (photo dated 2006)

SIMULACRUM AS RESEMBLANCE

In fact, pictographic or iconographic writing was not really a simple or direct system of resemblance: the hieroglyphs resemble the objects only in a limited, abstract way, and are transparent only to those trained in their conventions. Only the resemblance that is called a **simulacrum** can really invoke the original by perfecting duplicating it. For an example of what simulacrum is and how it works, let's discuss the Alfred Hitchcock movie *Vertigo* (1958). The movie opens with the protagonist, Scottie (James Stewart), unable to save a police officer from falling to his death from the roof of a tall building. This trauma causes him to suffer (the eponymous) vertigo, and is the core of the plot that follows. Scottie falls in love with Madeleine (Kim Novak), the wife of an important local man; but she is a troubled woman, obsessed with death, and apparently commits suicide. Scottie, desperate with grief and loss, finds a possible substitute for her in Judy. But where Madeleine is elegant and sophisticated, Judy is a loud shop girl. To make her the perfect copy, Scottie goes to considerable effort to remould her and form her into 'Madeleine'. She is not to be a substitute or resemblance, but a simulacrum: a perfect stand-in for the original, virtually indistinguishable from the source. Of course it doesn't work; but it is an interesting experiment in resemblance, simulacrum and the idea of presence – whether a sign can really make the original, real-world object present again.

The reason that no simulacrum can in fact perfectly stand in for the original is because there must always be a gap between the sign and what it signifies. Plato discussed this two millennia ago, in his argument that all we see and do is but a pale imitation of the ideal Form for the things we see and do, that exists in some transcendental realm, and is the origin for everything in our world of simulcra. Our efforts to produce representations or resemblances of that Form will only be partial and equivocal; and will be based on our prior understandings of what is important, of what something means, and of the right way of showing it. Scottie's attempt to reproduce Madeleine through a representation – Judy-the-simulacrum – failed not only because the Madeleine/Judy distinction was a trick, not only because there must be a gap between the sign and what it points to, but also because he did not really believe in the value of the outcomes.

ANALOGY AND SENSE

Even a perfect resemblance will be perfect only because it fits with ideas we might have about perfection, and about the thing it resembles. What is important here is that all uses of representation to make meaning are fundamentally epistemological. That is, they are not just about communicating something, but are based on theories of knowledge. There is no simple mirror of the world, but only ways of seeing that are inflected by philosophical and hence **ideological** perspectives. Slavoj Zizek argues that ideology is a 'generative matrix that regulates the relationship between visible and non-visible, between imaginable and non-imaginable' (1994: 1). We can only see, or make sense of what we see, on the basis of how we understand the world to be.

The world in medieval Europe was viewed through the epistemological filter of Christianity, so that it and all its contents were perceived as being there for a divine purpose (Eco 1986a: 53). Virtually everything one could see had a meaning based on some sort of resemblance to, or echo of, or analogy of, the divine: white meant light and goodness while black symbolized evil; lambs reminded viewers of Christ; doves were echoes of the holy spirit; olive branches indicated peace, and so on. Nor were Christians the only ones to make use of allegory. It was widely used in the ancient world: the image oppsite, for instance (Figure 1.2), is part of a fresco in Pompeii that is rich in elements that point to something beyond the everyday. Something similar still occurs, though more often in fun. Halloween imagery is an example of a cultural form that recalls the traditional logic of analogy: a pumpkin carved into a frightening mask, for instance, resembles an idea of the devil, and works best at night – the time of darkness and hence evil. The one in Figure 1.3 is carved

Figure 1.2 © Paul Travers 2006

Figure 1.3 © Paul Travers 2006

and lit so that it does something unexpected: the apparent image of pretty stars actually throws a demonic face against the wall.

As we saw in the case of hieroglyphics, the resemblance between the sign and the referent might be very slight, no more than an echo. But that was enough for the era, where what was required for meaning was not a sort of photographic reproduction, but a 'witty coincidence': just enough hints for someone to make a connection between the concrete and the abstract – the thing observed and the concept for which it stood. Resemblance, especially in the form of analogy (a lamb stands for Christ, for instance), was a way of filling the gap between the concrete and the abstract. There was never only one way of making analogies to fill that gap, though. Barbara Stafford writes that resemblance is an attempt to find sameness in difference (1999: 2): to see how a wavy line might be the same as a body of water, to see how a dove might be the same as God. It does recognize that things cannot precisely and perfectly represent other things, but suggests that there are ways of finding points of connection and association that help us to make sense of the world.

To do so we have to ignore the real differences, and look only for the possibility of sameness. For example, philosopher Adam Dickerson discusses how we read a smiley-face emoticon. The 'face' is on the one hand simply a combination of lines and dots, and on the other hand is itself and itself only. It is neither a resemblance nor a representation, because there is no actual smiley-face outside the picture that it might look like, or for which it is a substitute. Yet we can read it as both resemblance and representation. No one looks like a smiley-face; but the big smile on the emoticon sort of resembles a happy person. There is nothing outside the picture that is an original smiley-face which the emoticon can render in an image to make it present again, but there are happy people, and it stands for us as a valid representation (Dickerson 2004: 15). We know it is neither a face or a smiling face, simply a pattern of lines. We know it is not *in* the picture either – it *is* the picture; and yet we comfortably say that it is a face, smiling, in the picture; and it is a picture of smile. It is nonsense, and yet it makes perfectly good sense. And it spirals on to make sense of other nonsense objects. This manhole cover (Figure 1.4), for instance, looks like someone winking, someone almost but not quite smiling, someone who is present. And yet all it is, is a chunk of metal on a Paris street, covered in litter.

The smiley-face is similar in its properties to pictographic writing: it gives a direct reflection of things that are in the world. But the signs Eco identifies as medieval representations of God rely on a different logic of resemblance. Here the resemblance is not a sort of mirror image, but a resemblance of affinity, or sympathy – based on connection and not of reflection. We find this in images and also in spoken or written language. Philosopher John Searle, for instance, points out that if you say someone is tall, he or she is tall only

Figure 1.4   A manhole cover, Paris (2006)

as an attribution, not a reality (1993: 86–7). Every person, after all, is short in real or actual terms, when say, compared with a giraffe – even a giraffe who is short in giraffe terms. But a person short in actual terms may well be tall in relational terms: a women who measures two meters – short in comparison with giraffes – is tall by human standards: a women who measures only 2.5 meters is tall in relation to toddlers.

ANALOGY AND EDUCATION

This is a mode of language use that is more closely associated with affect – feelings, attitudes – than with deductive reason. It is figurative rather than factual, and more inclined to communicate through story than through evidence and argument. It is thus a system of communication that is very well-suited to teaching. In the Medieval period the focus on seeing everything as an analogy for the divine served as a reminder to people about the centrality of their religion to their lives. In a similar way, experts often use analogy – resemblance – to explain complex issues to those who do not know their field of expertise.

Writings by early medical scientists are full of analogical explanations and descriptions of the human body and how it works. The pelvic cavity was often described as a cave, and this allowed listeners – students, other doctors – to visualize its form and to be alert to important issues for research or examination (*it is dark in there; there may be unexpected tunnels or fissures; go carefully!*). Following the same principle of rendering visible something that is hidden and complex, people using language to persuade will often use analogy. For example, environmentalists will talk of the 'rape' of the earth, an analogy that brings to mind vulnerable femininity, brute force, violation, and the need for people of goodwill and legal integrity to intervene. These are not 'true' images in the sense used by deductive reasoning, and nor are they 'true' – mirror image – resemblances, but they are pointers to something that a speaker might wish to posit as true.

IDEOLOGY AND RESEMBLANCE

It is important to remember that all resemblances, and indeed all representations, are only partial and contingent. We interpret signs in order to extract a desired truth. In Victorian England there was a tradition of using an extensive range of images (signs) on gravestones to tell something important about their beliefs. A number of graves in London's Highgate Cemetery, for example, are adorned with carvings of guttering candles. This is a sign that reminds viewers of the transitory nature of life. There is no reason it should necessarily do so; after all, a candle, however low it has burned, looks nothing like a dying person. The only likeness is one of connection – both are dying. And even in what might seem to be the most naturalistic, the most mimetic, form of communication, that of onomatapoeia, cultural differences far override whatever might be the actuality of the referent. In France, for instance, barking dogs make a sound rendered as *ouaoua*; in Anglophone societies the same sound is rendered '*woof*', or '*yap*' (Belsey 1980: 41). The French and the English both, I assume, hear their dogs as 'naturally' making those very different sounds – even hear the same dog making those very different sounds. So what an individual person sees or hears as 'natural' is in fact cultural: it is the effect of ideological and epistemological frameworks.

Think, for instance, of modern public signage, which is a system of communication based on resemblance. The idea is that it acts as a perfect form of communication, that because it is 'obvious' and directly mimetic it can be read by anyone. It is not quite as simple as that. Look, for example, at what is a very common sign in public spaces around the globe (Figure 1.5). The pictures of figures on the doors of public conveniences are recognizable as male or female by very abstract, crude outlines – females in skirts, males in trousers. 'Obviously' these resemble men and women – and yet they don't in any real way. Men's and women's bodies are far more complicated than these line drawings. They are also more cultured than natural, so the signs do not just

Figure 1.5 Public Signage (2005)

say 'men', 'women', but men and women of a particular period, and in a particular society. In many cultures, for instance, men wear skirts and women wear trousers, in a reversal of the conventional (Western) sign. But whatever icons are chosen to stand in for men and women, there is always more being conveyed than gender: epistemology and ideology are also being conveyed. For instance, this gender differentiation on the doors of public toilets naturalizes the social norm that, regardless of how we organize our facilities at home, men and women must use separate conveniences in public. The signs also naturalize the norm that only certain parts of the anatomy may be seen. Heads, legs and arms are visible, but the actual markers of bodily difference – breasts, male genitalia – are not shown. Such markers would, in fact, offer much more explicit statements of who should enter which room, but cultural norms that prohibit the representation of nudity are overcome by representational convenience. The images resemble human male and female figures, but – like the baroque 'witty coincidence' – only just.

THE BIRTH OF MODERNITY

Resemblance in its various forms pretty much dominated seeing and making meanings up to the period of **the Enlightenment**, after which representation became the more dominant mode (Foucault 1970: 51). The Enlightenment is the beginning of the modern age; it was characterized by a massive outpouring of philosophical thought and political actions, all grounded on a belief in what is 'rational, secular, democratic, and universal' (Alves 2000: 488). 'Rational' means that reason, rather than belief or tradition, became the basis for engaging with ideas and concepts; 'secular' because the Church finally lost its temporal power and human thought, rather than God, became the measure of truth; 'democratic' because it also saw the shift from rule by the elites to elected governments; and 'universal' because the freedoms to be ushered in by the Century of Lights were for all. Consequently, Alves writes, 'Man was, therefore, the subject and mastermind of history' (2000: 488). And it was 'man', rather than woman, who became this free subject; though Enlightenment thought laid the foundations for the liberation of women as well as men, it took a couple more centuries before women even won the right to vote.

With the emergence of the modern era, science emerged as a positivist system of observation, testing and measurement; pragmatic reason replaced mysticism, resulting in what Max Weber termed 'the disenchantment of the world'; and a bright new period of human history seemed to have begun. Of course it wasn't only positive: by the nineteenth century many commentators were pointing out qualifications on the promise of the Enlightenment. Marx, for instance, wrote about the pressures on individuals, and the limits on their freedoms (though Man as a concept may be the centre of the world, individual men and women are not); Nietzsche pointed out the irrationality and particularity of what was 'reason' and 'universalism'; and then the grand narratives of the Enlightenment were blown apart on the battlefields of the First World War. It turned out that rather than being 'truth', the philosophical pillars of modernity were just another set of perspectives.

This is the basis for our contemporary understandings of representation. Claire Colebrook writes that modernity ushered in representation because it countered the old approach, where knowledge about something was grounded on and validated by direct and immediate reference to the thing itself. With the new view of science, knowledge about something was grounded on and validated by representations: arguments, diagrams, pictures and other forms that were separated from the thing itself (Colebrook 2000: 49). In this way modern science changed the world from a place of mystery and habitation into an object of study. It also changed the way of looking at, framing and naming the world: it carved a space between the thing observed and the observer, between an experience and how it is articulated; it initiated the practice of mediation.

This was not, of course, the first time mediation was used. Human beings have always observed and named the things in their environment, and have used marks and sounds of various sorts to bring into presence an absent object or an idea. So a fundamental principle of representation – the act of *standing in for* – has always been around. People in the ancient world had words for the creature we know as a cat that would have been every bit as arbitrary as c-a-t; inevitably: communication would be impossible if one needed to carry around an actual cat in order to talk about it. Even if were it possible to carry that cat around on the off-chance that the topic of cats might come up in conversation, the principle of representation would still apply because the cat I show to people would change from being *this particular cat* to being the sign of cat, standing in for all cats, and for the idea of cat-ness. In other words, as soon as people began to communicate, they began to make representations – to use signs that stood in for the things being discussed. But how they figured and understood the relationship between the concrete thing and its sign has differed over human history.

FROM RESEMBLANCE TO REPRESENTATION

The move from resemblance to representation was a move from a system of meaning-making based on similitude to one based on difference. The issue of similitude – or its capacity to mirror reality – was seen as a problem by many philosophers of the Enlightenment and after. The main issue was that a sign that resembled a real-world object or event seemed to imply that it contained the truth of that object or event: that it possessed the presence it was now re-presenting. In fact, as we discussed above, there was no real likeness or empirical resemblance, just ideas of likeness or association. But this was not enough.

René Descartes, the philosopher Michel Foucault identifies as the first important exponent of what we now understand as representation, opposed resemblance on the basis that it offers only false comparisons and, as I pointed out above, tends to work through the emotions rather than through reason. Descartes writes:

> Whenever men notice some similarity between two things, they are wont to ascribe to each, even in those respects in which the two differ, what they have found to be true of the other. Thus, they erroneously compare the sciences, which entirely consist in the cognitive exercise of the mind, with disposition of the body. (1969: 359–60)

He is prepared to allow resemblance as a basis for lived experience, but insists that it is inadequate for the development of science or reason. He was not the first to make this point; we find a similar complaint in Plato's *The Republic*, where he criticizes art for doing just this, presenting illusions as actualities, and seducing people on the basis of emotion rather than reasoned thought.

But Descartes' call to reject resemblance in favour of representation does more than simply separate emotion and reason. It also encourages a change in the grounds of perception and discussion – from the visual to the linguistically based, as Martin Jay suggests (1993: 79). This is taking us at least two steps from the thing being represented: not only is it removed by being turned into image, but it is removed again by being reduced to words, and to an ever-increasing abstraction, accompanied by an ever-increasing distance between people and their physical environment.

REPRESENTATION AND REALITY?

Can representation deliver the rational truth that was at the heart of Enlightenment thought? Certainly it can allow us to consider and discuss what 'rational truth' means, or how we understand the world to be arranged. Frank Ankersmit explains this phenomenon as follows:

> one of the reasons why we need representations is that they enable us to obtain and to express an insight into the nature of things. That is why we have artistic representation, historical representation and political representation. But elsewhere representation is no less important. For representation defines reality; and that is why we could not possibly do without it. (2003: 320)

'Representation defines reality': it tells us what it is. But it does much more than that; it also makes and shapes our understanding of reality. We can know and access the world only through language, or representation.

We know of the Renaissance, for instance, because of how it has been represented, and the features of that period that historians have identified and written about. There is, though, nothing 'real' about the Renaissance in any way other than in how aspects of the period have been categorized; so, Ankersmit continues, '"things" such as the Renaissance could not even be said to *exist* in the absence of their representations' (2003: 322). Artist Paul Carter writes, similarly, of how Australia came into being as far as the Western world was concerned: 'Before it was known, Australia was named. Before it was seen, it was represented' (2004: 1). Long before Captain Cook reached the shores or circumnavigated the continent, even before the early Dutch explorers had bumped into bits of Australia, European cartographers had drafted an unknown landmass more or less in the vicinity occupied by Australia. Of course it was already known by indigenous Australians and their neighbours, but their knowledge and systems of framing the place were very different from that of the European explorers and colonists. It is hardly surprising, then, that the British who occupied Australia failed not only to see ('see') Aboriginal Australians, but failed to see Australia from the indigenous perspective; they already 'knew' it, long before they actually experienced it, thanks to the various representations made of it well before the first fleet arrived in 1788. So:

> Reality is in the eye of the beholder; or rather, what is regarded as real depends on how reality is defined by a particular social group. ... reality may be in the eye of the beholder, but the eye has had a cultural training, and is located in a social setting and a history. (Kress and van Leeuwen 1996: 163)

Just as our particular cultural history sets the terms for how we will represent and thus make our reality, so too that history, and its modes of representation, make each of us what we are. When I am represented, socially or politically, I am subtly or explicitly changed by that representation, because I am separated from myself and made to see myself, as it were, at a distance. When I am invoked by political candidates representing me, it is not me that I observe in their representations, but an abstract idea I do not recognize as myself. The person disappears in, or is blurred by, the idea of the electorate.

This effect is perhaps even more obvious in the case of photographs, as Kate Bowles describes (2002: 73), especially photos of the self. A photo may remind you of an event, but it does not take you there – not literally. And moreover, while it is 'you', at one level, it is not really you. If you look at it, you might say or think 'that's me'. Your mother might show the picture to friends and say: 'This is my child'. It is not you, nor your mother's child. It is a photograph, merely the capturing on paper of light and shade, line and point, at a particular moment and in a particular place. Nor does it really look like you, to you: for one thing, we experience the world from the inside out, looking out through the holes in our skulls. When looking at a photograph of me, I experience the world looking in, from the outside: something that is pretty disturbing if I think about it to any extent. A second problem is that I know myself only in mirror image – what I see when I look in the mirror. A photograph reverses this. For example, I have a mole under my left eye; I know it is the left because I can touch it. But in my mirror reflection it is on the right hand side. When I see photos of myself, I look subtly wrong – the mole is on the 'wrong' side (not the side I see from the inside out, but the side the world sees, from the outside in). This disconnection, this dislocation, is explored in a poem by Canadian writer Margaret Atwood, titled 'This is a photograph of me'. The poem describes a landscape, and the lake in that landscape, and then continues:

> I am in the lake, in the center
> of the picture, just under the surface.
> It is difficult to say where
> precisely, or to say
> how large or small I am ...' (1983: 1373–4)

The poem is consciously unsettling. Although it is written in the first person, and in the present tense, it describes the photograph as having been 'taken/the day after I drowned' – a logical impossibility, but a worrying conceit. It circles around ideas of loss, absence and exclusion. The line breaks insert a halting quality to the sentence, as though the speaker is fumbling with language. It also talks explicitly about the problem of meaning – the photograph is 'blurred', for instance: it cannot produce the truth of its title.

Gilles Deleuze explains this uncomfortable experience by referring to the idea of representation as a mirror. This is not the mirror of resemblance (similitude) but the mirror of difference. Take, for instance, your own name: it is you, and at the same time it is not you, but just a collection of alphabetical shapes or uttered sounds. You (the thing itself) and your name (the designation that stands in for you) simply circulate:

> It is a two-sided entity, equally present in the signifying and the signified series. ... Thus, it is at once word and thing, name and object, sense and *denotatum*, expression and designation, etc. It guarantees, therefore, the convergence of the two series which it traverses but precisely on the condition that it makes them endlessly diverge. It has the property of always being displaced in relation to itself. (Deleuze 1990: 48)

In photographs, in our names, and in political representation we are always present and not present, always weaving back and forth between our **phenomenological** sense of ourselves, and our having been reduced to a sign.

VARIOUS SIGNAGE

I pointed out in the Introduction that there are several meanings of the term 'representation'; let me detail them a bit further to explain how it functions as a game. When we refer to texts, representation may be understood as transitive: that is, a representation *represents something*. It may also be understood as reflexive: that is, a representation *presents itself representing something*. It may be an instance of substitution, the making present of something that is absent; it may be a matter not of substitution, but of intensified *presentation*. Louis Marin explains this in his discussion of the effect that can be produced by visual representations of royalty. In discussing a trompe-l'oil in the Sun King's palace, the 'Ambassador's Staircase', Marin shows that the ostensible subject, the Ambassador (an important person, the delegate of a foreign king) is reduced, by the structure of the painting, to a mere object: 'the gazer gazed upon. The spectator has become a spectacle' (2001: 318). It is the king who gazes upon all, and is also the subject of everyone else's gaze, not as object, but as intensified representation. Marin goes on to say that in this respect:

All representation, all mimesis, is, in a sense, royal or theoretical: with it is instituted ... a subject who dominates appearances, thereby appropriating it for himself and identifying himself as a truth-judging subject in that appropriation. (2001: 318)

The subject of the painting is represented in the work, but at the same time is self-representing: the painted face looks back at the viewer, controlling the interchange. It is the work of representation performing communication through presentation. The portrait instantiates a reality because it represents not only a human being, but also a political situation – the actual status of the king compared with the subject-viewer – and because it demands particular responses from those in its presence.

Marin also points to a third, and older, use of the term representation – 'to appear in person and exhibit things'. This he draws from Furetière's Dictionary (published 1690) where one of the meanings of representation is given as being 'to present oneself representing something' (Marin 2001: 352). This, the reflexive dimension of representation, is a reminder that there is usually an active investment in representation; someone makes something, and stands in the place of an absence, bringing both themselves and the represented thing or person to 'life'. An extreme version of this would be the situation where the person performing the representation is actually representing themselves in themselves, rather than through an image – a purely reflexive, and not a transitive mode. An example of this might be when the British royal family or the Pope emerge on their respective balconies, to be seen. They are themselves, individual human beings. They are there as representatives not only of themselves, but also of their office. And they are both presenting and *re*presenting themselves. This involves a curious doubling of the self (*this* me is representing *that* me); it also reduces the person from self to representation: a distance, an abstraction, which is at the heart of representation.

This outline of some uses of representation does not, of course, draw attention to the modes of representation, or the media in which they are communicated to us. But media have a huge effect on how something is communicated, what it can mean, and the functions a representation might perform. Paintings, books, music, design, performances – each might take precisely the same issue, and communicate it entirely differently, with very different effects, simply because of the impact of the medium being used. Digital media make this very evident, because in the digital environment the 'language' of representation is entirely central to how, and whether, a text works (Buzzetti 2002). Think, for instance, of the writing of this page you are reading. A human being thought up the words, and used an alphabetical system and a language well established in history. Those words had to be keyed into a computer using a software program that digitised – or converted – them into a string of characters that are resistant to swift, fluent reading (by those not familiar with computer language). The computer screen showed the words in a way that reproduced the analogue equivalent to the digital coding. The digital material remained hidden behind the screen: this is the material that allowed the disc that contained this final, edited manuscript to be read by a digital printer, and turned out as a book in conventional, readable English. For computers, representation must be, first of all, digital. Without this precondition, it cannot function. But computers do not use representation the way we do as humans. A digital representaion is a representation 'for' as well as a representation 'of': it is a sign that is not a sign, designed not simply for communication but for storage and manipulation.

Still, this usage can be subverted in a way that renders digital text – code – as 'pure' representation. The Australian media artist Mary-Anne Breeze ('Mez') does precisely this in her 'codework' poems, an example of which can be found at http://beehive.temporalimage.com/archive/5larc.html (accessed 13 September 2007). Titled_ [ad] [Dressed in a Skin C.ode_, the work uses the complexities and inaccessibility of computer code to point out the ambiguities and sheer chance of much representation. It uses the representational devices of a computer to generate a work of art, an instance of representation that is as much about feeling as communicating, and that critically engages with the very act of making representation.

Gilles Deleuze identifies a similar complexity in human representation. He makes the point that regardless of the use, the mode or the medium of representation, meaning-making is not just a matter of a circular process – from utterance towards actualities and back to other utterances. In fact he suggests it is not circular, but that the two domains of propositions (utterances) and actualities (things) are themselves like two circles that may or may not touch. It is not *reality* that is brought into presence through representation; rather, it is *meaning* that is brought to light. People align the borders of the representations and that actualities to make meaning happen, and to make it seem real. We construct meaning out of the raw materials that are on the one hand the world, and on the hand, statements about the world.

REPRESENTATION MAKES MEANING

So, the processes of representation do not simply make meaning present; rather, they *construct* that meaning. And certainly people seem eager to make meanings: indeed, as Simon Critchley writes, 'there is an almost irresistible desire to stuff the world full of meaning' (2004: xxiii–xxiv). We find meanings in the most unlikely or subtle of things – a sunset, for instance, which in fact signifies nothing of itself, but is used as a sign of the end of the day, as a metaphor for romance, for the end of things, or for the completion of a legal contract. A sunset does not 'mean' per se; it is not an artefact designed for meaning but a physical phenomenon. Still, we make it mean.

We also make each other 'mean', in a similar way, because we read people's minds – that is, we name the state of someone else's mind based on how we perceive their actions, and what we think those actions mean (Baron-Cohen 1995). Someone is slowly shredding a tissue; very well, then they must be bored or tense. Someone smiles widely; very well, then they must be happy or excited. Someone flinches away from a sudden movement; very well, then they must be afraid, or stressed. Someone takes a slice of cake from the plate on the table; very well, then they must want something sweet to eat. And so on. Our mind-reading may be spot on; or it may diverge wildly from what the person is actually thinking and feeling. But in any event, as research in the cognitive sciences shows, it is something that most people do, mostly quite accurately, and mostly without giving it a great deal of conscious thought.

Their doing it, though, can make it (appear) 'real'. Deleuze uses the notion of displacement to elaborate the uncertain or unstable nature of identity. With every new designation, he writes, the 'two series' (signified and signifier; me and how I am represented) may diverge in a different way. For example, following the 2001 attacks on New York and Washington and the USA's return attack on Afghanistan, a number of media reports focused on the history of the connection between Afghanistan and the West: Britain's long and unsuccessful struggle to hold Afghanistan, and the similarly long and unsuccessful attempt made by the Soviet Union, were revised as evidences of the intractability of the Afghan region and the stubborn resistance of Afghan people. It was difficult to 'read' Afghanistan in any other way than as the home of cunning, determined resistance fighters, a place of craggy impossible terrain, where locals are able to beat back considerably more sophisticated armies by virtue of local knowledge and determination. The 'truth' of the Afghan people became entrenched – at least until the next way of representing them emerges in the discourse.

Behind the urge to make meaning is what Jacques Derrida calls the '**metaphysics of presence**'. We saw above that the central concerns of the Enlightenment were reason and truth, because of the idea that these would set people free from the yoke of tradition, religion and ignorance. Enlightenment thought aimed to disenchant the world – to remove the magic by showing how things really worked, to allow us to understand and thus control our environments. It lifted human beings away from the domain of nature, and into the somewhat disembodied realm of culture where reason and clear thought were the watchwords.

Enlightenment discourse, though, typically ignored the fact that the whole logic of this new system of knowledge shared aspects of the magical, traditional mode of metaphysics. Metaphysics is a branch of philosophy traditionally concerned with the nature of the world. More typically, the term is used for what we might call 'the unseen things'. Like the modern scientist, the metaphysician wanted to discover the essence of all things. Of course the traditional mode did not use the sophisticated methods of science, or ensure replicability of results; it was closer to religion than to science. But both metaphysics and science are grounded on the belief that there are secrets in the universe that can be uncovered and discovered; that it is possible to understand, and give an account of, reality (Ankersmit 2003: 317).

THE ORIGINS OF THE SIGN

Just as metaphysics lurks in the domain of science, so too it inflects the domain of representation. It is important to understand this because it goes some way towards explaining the complexities of this system. A reference that is grounded in the real world – say, one based on resemblance – has a very different ontology (being) from one that is purely symbolic. The one based on resemblance is only one step away from the thing itself, and remains closely bound to it. But a representative sign is at least twice separated from the thing itself, as I pointed out in the Introduction. Its connection with the referent is arbitrary; which is to say, it is not grounded in any actual association between sign and signified. Still, to say that a representation stands in, or is a substitute for the original, implies that the original is capable of being made present – and that it is a convincing and necessary source of the sign. Richard van Oort points out:

> Any reasonably complete account of representation must sooner or later address the problem of origins. Where do our representations come from, and how are they grounded in the real physical and biological world? (2003: 245)

This is an important question because it goes to the heart of the connection between the representation and the original. It is also a question that could only be asked by someone in the modern age, because it shows the drive, since the Enlightenment, to understand how the world fits together in a logical and rational fashion. But like other aspects of Enlightenment thought – science, for instance – it keeps one foot in the enchanted world of pre-modernity.

GROUNDING METAPHORS

The contemporary notion of symbolic representation, as I suggested in the Introduction and will develop further in the next chapter, is that the representative signs are abstract and arbitrary. But alongside this dominant notion of the arbitrary, abstract nature of the sign is another that takes a very different view. This is the belief that though signs may vary from culture to culture, they are not arbitrary, because they come from actual experience in the physical and social world.

The writers most often cited in discussions about this are George Lakoff and Mark Johnson, authors of a seminal text on metaphor. They argue that 'the essence of metaphor is understanding and experiencing one kind of thing in terms of another' (Lakoff and Johnson 1980: 5): in other words, metaphor belongs in the category of substitutionary representation. Such representation, they go on to write, emerges from real-world, observed phenomena – things we see, things we feel – that are then turned into metaphors and gradually move away from direct to purely analogical connection. All our metaphors and hence all our ways of making meaning through representation, they suggest, depend on those real-world events that become 'grounding metaphors'.

They use the example 'Harry is in the kitchen' to explain this (Lakoff and Johnson 1980: 59). Harry is a real-world person, who can be perceptually observed in an actual place. To say he is 'in the kitchen' is not metaphorical, but a simple description. If rendered as a painting it would be pure resemblance. That description, though, provides us with the notion of a container for Harry, and this notion can be abstracted from the real-world perceptual domain to a more metaphorical one. We can then say, for instance, that 'Harry is in love'. Of course Harry is not *in* a physical container called 'love' as he was *in* a physical container called 'the kitchen', but the idea of *being in* carries through. This second container is more abstract; you could not paint a picture of Harry in love that would simply and without additional information resemble 'love' – unlike that previously mentioned painting that would directly resemble a man in a kitchen. Someone standing in a space is in the realm of phenomenology; someone 'in love' is in the nature of an abstraction and so cannot belong to the realm of resemblance.

Lakoff and Johnson's argument, then, is that the perception of a real-world phenomenon can, if it becomes a grounding metaphor, provide a basis for genuinely representational – that is, arbitrary and abstract – communication. Every time we use the term 'in' to describe someone's state of mind or other condition, lurking behind it is the real-world, perceptual and sensual sense of an enclosed space.

This notion of representation through metaphor – a very widely-held one – is closely committed to the metaphysics of presence. It implies that all the terms of our representation are based in an actuality, and that behind the veil of the representation the reality can be glimpsed, if you just look carefully. As van Oort complains:

> this explanation of how metaphors are grounded in the real world is really no explanation because it assumes precisely what is at issue, namely, the difference between a symbolic reference system and a reference system based on perceptual categorization. (2003: 246)

This is not to say that perception and representation are never connected, or that there are not good precedents for this approach to understanding the origins of language. Michel Foucault described something very similar in his *The Order of Things* where he discusses the origin of writing as being first of all based on resemblance, then on metaphors linked to resemblances, and finally on symbolic writing which also uses resemblance, to a more 'concealed' extent (though he is speaking here of a more pictographic than alphabetic form of writing). He goes on to state:

> Originally everything had a name – a proper or peculiar name. Then the name became attached to a single element of the thing, and became applicable to all the other individual things that also contained that element: it is no longer a particular oak that is called tree, but anything that includes at least a trunk and branches. The name also became attached to a conspicuous circumstance: night came to designate, not the end of this particular day, but the period of darkness separating all sunsets from all dawns. Finally, it attached itself to analogies: everything was called a leaf that was as thin and flexible as the leaf of a tree. (1970: 110–11)

So finally, from the word 'leaf' being the name for a single and particular object, it gradually comes to designate sheets of paper, fine pastry, room partitions, as well as every instance of foliage. Fair enough; and at one level it seems that Foucault is mining the same territory as Lakoff and Johnson. But unlike those scholars, for whom linguistic representation remains at base phenomenological, Foucault insists that words are in fact free to align in many ways and to stand in for many possible real-world phenomena, whether there is a causal relationship between the word and the phenomenon or not.

UNGROUNDED REPRESENTATIONS

Often, there is no such relationship. Film-maker Danny Boyle, in an interview about his movie *Sunshine* (2007), talked about the pleasures of making a film about the sun because of its importance to us all: it is, he said, the source of life, and that is why people have treated it as a god. This is a matter of assuming a relationship on the basis of common sense; it is a very common assumption and does seem perfectly reasonable. But drawing a line from sun, to source of life, to worship begins at the wrong end of things, because it assumes that the worship is the result of people knowing the sun's life-giving properties. But there is no real evidence that sun worshippers understood the place of that star in the solar system. Sociologist Emile Durkheim (1965) made this point decades ago, and it still applies to virtually anything people have viewed as possessing symbolic significance. His argument was that people perceive things as being awe-inspiring not because of the phenomenal properties of these things, but because of the representations their culture has made of them. This is why one real-world thing may be perceived, observed and invested with symbolic significance, and another is barely, or not at all, observed: a culture will worship the sun, but not the ocean; or a mountain, but not the sun. If our systems of representation genuinely rested firmly on real-world perceptions, we might expect there to be some consistency across cultures in what they observe and how they structure thought: yet 'it is precisely the functional explanation of this transition that cannot be reduced to purely biological terms' (van Oort 2003: 244).

The issue for van Oort is that Lakoff and Johnson's dependence on perception overlooks the fact that symbolic representation is disconnected from actuality. There is a significant difference between a reference that is grounded in the real world and one that is purely symbolic. This is, of course, another way of describing the problem of representation as a problem of the metaphysics of presence: Lakoff and Johnson depend entirely on the prior existence of real-world events and effects that provide the 'grounding metaphor' on which all other metaphors are based, and from which they emerge.

Their thesis depends on there being a real relationship between perception and meaning-making – as though perception were a simple practice that anyone could do in much the same way. But as Henri Bergson points out, this is simply not the case. Perception is cultural and specific, limited and interested. Bergson uses the concept of nothingness to explain his point: most of us have a sense of what is meant by 'nothing': it is absence, emptiness, it is a vast space that is unfilled. 'But in reality there is no vacuum. We perceive and can only perceive occupied space. One thing disappears only because another replaces it' (Bergson 1946: 97). So we might think we can perceive nothingness, but it is not a vacuum, not just absence. Rather what we actually perceive is presence and changing perspectives on the presence.

THE GAME OF PRESENCE

Much of Derrida's writing has taken on the connection between reality and representation, and shown that the apparent connection is generally just an effect of relations of power. If I can convince people that the sun is a divinity, and that we must therefore worship it; and, moreover, that I myself have special insights about its nature and how it wants to be worshipped, I will have the tools to control much of the discourse and practice in my community. This is a crude example, and I do not suggest that it is the primary origin for sun worship or even a conscious point of origin; but nonetheless, once a system of sun worship was in place, it was very easy to use it to manage the population.

The metaphysics of presence underpinned the power of images and other representations of the sun, implying that the actual presence, with all its might and authority, lay behind and backed up the representations.

Other scholars have taken a similar line to Derrida, investigating the apparent link between representation and reality, and pointing out its very tenuous nature. Claire Colebrook (2000), in her insightful essay into the philosophical quarrels that surround representation, suggests that rather than relying on the metaphysics of presence, we should recognize that representation is not a mirror of the world, but simply a human practice, an effect of being in the world. We experience the world as given, or 'just there', not as represented or mirrored. Drawing on Deleuze, she suggests we consider the possibility that the world is not present, in the sense of being presented to us, and subsequently re-presented by us. Rather, it is we who are in it, at all times. The representations we make do not affirm the presence of real-world phenomena, but are simply effects of our being in the world. Like Derrida, Deleuze rejects the metaphysics of presence, or of presence at all in representation. Representation does not, for these thinkers, bring the idea of the real-world event into language, but is simply an effect of that real-world event (Deleuze 1991: 30). And the language in which we articulate it does not bring about a re-presentation – a substitution – but is something else entirely – a game of language played by members of society.

GETTING IT WRONG

Given that meaning and reality are made, they clearly do not simply or innocently exist. There is an actor (a series of actors) behind every instance of representation. And in every instance of representation, a different perspective may be offered on the item under discussion. In some cases what happens is termed *mis-* (or wrong) representation. This is a tricky issue; as I have discussed above, representation does not provide either presence or truth. How can we say something is a misrepresentation if its obverse, perfect representation, does not exist?

We call a representation wrong when we don't approve of the reason for the representation; when we believe it is designed to convince us unfairly, to con us or to pull the wool over our eyes. Advertising is the field that attracts many of the complaints about misrepresentation, not surprisingly because, like politics, advertising is interested in producing a very specific image of its products. In advertisements for British tourism designed for overseas customers, for instance, the scenes are usually of grand old buildings, beautiful green parks, or splendid craggy hills. I have seen these things when I've been a tourist in Britain; but I have also seen many, many sights that never make it into the advertising campaigns, and that in fact would be likely to put me off coming to Britain for a holiday. I could, I suppose, write to British Tourism to complain about misrepresentation because they did not show that St. Paul's seems in variably to be hidden under great sheets of canvas, make explicit the numbers of beggars on city streets, or explain how rarely the sun shines.

But this would not be playing the game correctly. The issue at stake is not really misrepresentation, but 'interested' representation: representation that offers only a particular *inflection* of that situation. Of course Britain has wonderful buildings, parks and countryside. It might be fair to argue that a more representative image of the UK would show economically depressed areas, people struggling with cold and rain, littered streets and so on; but that would not be a 'true' representation either, just a different one. Any advertiser will edit out everything unlikely to sell, say, tourist destinations; and even if an advertiser were struck by the need to provide a fully balanced representation of the nation, there would never be time to show all its facets. Partial, contingent representations are the best we can achieve.

This is not to say that we all tell the truth to the best of our (limited) ability all the time. While misrepresentation might not be the best term to explain what can go wrong, there are examples of deliberate efforts to mislead through representation. Mistakes can be made, of course; some articulations are less clear and precise than others; and insufficient or flawed data might have been used. But beyond that, sometimes people deliberately offer misleading representations. There are outright lies; and there is also what Princeton University's professor of moral philosophy, Harry Frankfurt, terms 'bullshit' (2005).

Frankfurt acknowledges that it is never possible to communicate the full truth – that, indeed, 'every use of language without exception has some, but not all, of the characteristics of lies' (2005: 9) – but goes on to draw a distinction between lies and what he calls bullshit, or humbug. 'Humbug' is Max Black's term for representation made with 'an intention to deceive' (Frankfurt 2005: 7). The assertions by US president George W Bush, UK prime minister Tony Blair and Australian prime minister John Howard in the early 2000s that weapons of mass destruction had been found in Iraq, and that Iraq was a hotbed of Al Quada terrorism, are examples of 'humbug'. Knowing it was not true, those leaders presented their assertions as true with the intention, if not to deceive their publics, certainly to persuade them to support the invasion of Iraq. One might assume that once the intelligence community had shown them – and the public – the contrary evidence, they would have realized that public trust was at stake, but each went on to focus on the game of politics rather than the actuality of the facts.

What matters in this sort of situation is not that a politician is in fact trustworthy, or is in fact trusted, but that he is able to represent himself in the place of something called 'trust'. What the politician wants is for his audience:

to think of him as a patriot, as someone who has deep thoughts and feelings about the origins and the mission of our [sic] country, who appreciates the importance of religion, who is sensitive to the greatness of our history, whose pride in that history is combined with humility before God, and so on. (Frankfurt 2005: 18)

There is a fine line, in Frankfurt's account, between lies and bullshit, though both could be termed misrepresentation. A liar believes that the thing he is saying is not true; a bullshitter doesn't care whether it is true or not, only that it lets him advance in the game (Frankfurt 2005: 34). The point about bullshit is that the person making the representation is concerned 'to deceive us about his enterprise. His only indispensably distinctive characteristic is that in a certain way he misrepresents what he is up to' (Frankfurt 2005: 53). Both the liar and the truth-teller share an interest in and a concern for the truth. The bullshitter does not.

Perhaps in this respect we can say that the tourism advertisements I described above are bullshit, rather than a lie: they are not concerned with whether their representations are true, only that they will effectively convince tourists to visit the sites they are selling. A con artist, on the other hand, is more likely to be an actual liar: he will be concerned with the truth, and with concealing it.

It really isn't valid, or useful, to talk about misrepresentation as though there were a correct representation against which we could measure it. Certainly lies and bullshit can be demonstrated to be inaccurate, inappropriate or otherwise flawed; but we can never 'get it right' as far as representation is concerned; we can only gather information and mount an argument in the way that best serves our purposes; and hopefully those will be ethical purposes. No text is a vessel sufficiently large to contain all the possible meanings that can be made of it, or all the effects it might have. There are always latent meanings, and latent effects; even in the smallest statement. Think of that famous joke:

'Time flies'
'You can't; they fly too fast'

Despite these difficulties, we all make representations all the time, without necessarily thinking consciously about how to do it. Our capacity to reduce the world to signs and to use those signs fluently, or to treat a substitute as validly standing in for an absent original, is remarkable. In the next chapter I will develop these issues by focusing on how representation works in language, and how its particular abstractions and chains of signs allow us to make and to represent ideas about the world.

2 Language and representation

Language is, in the opinion of many theorists, what makes us human. It makes us – that is, *constructs* us – in a very real sense because to be a member of society, and hence recognized as a person, you must have access to language. The language we speak, how we speak it, with what accent, what fluency and what content, determines who we can be in the world, and sets in motion a series of ideas, knowledges and attitudes about and for us. Do we use it, or does it use us?

WHAT IS LANGUAGE?

This sounds a little ridiculous, I know; after all, language has no agency or identity of its own. It is a social artefact, a tool made by human beings for human use. But how we relate to it is unclear, as W.S. Graham evokes in these lines:

What is the language using us for?
I don't know. Have the words ever
Made anything of you, near a kind
Of truth you thought you were? Me
Neither. The words like albatrosses
Are only a doubtful touch towards
My going and you lifting your hand
To speak to illustrate an observed
Catastophe(1975: 44).

The albatross in the lines here is a reference to Coleridge's poem, 'The Ancient Mariner'. Having killed an albatross, against all the rules of the sea, the Mariner is condemned to wear it as a dead weight around his neck, and spend the rest of time telling his incomprehensible and tedious tale. The poem and the story of the Ancient Mariner are both wonderful analogies for the bleaker aspect of language: the fact that we cannot escape its rules, the compulsion we are under to use it, work it and rework it constantly, the role it plays as both social glue and social repellant. 'What is the language using us for?/I don't know': and yet it does use us as vehicles. It also lets us down, it does not give us the truth we expected, it does not even give us the connection we hoped for (just the 'doubtful touch' in a moment of parting; just the hand 'lifted to speak', but not managing to express that 'observed catastrophe').

Most of the time we don't think about what it is, what it means to us, or how we use it, although it is one of the more complex things we humans do. Linguists, neurologists and philosophers, though, wrestle with how people are able to pluck abstractions out of the air, and turn them into meaning, and how we manage to code a massive range of possibilities in a way that renders them (more or less) intelligible to most other people. As I described in the previous chapter, we use language to convey what we think truth is, what actualities exist and what possibilities there might be; and yet language is not a thing as such. It is the material in which we describe the concrete, but is itself entirely ephemeral: a system of communication and meaning-making, and not an object or identity.

Language works through a process that involves using signs to stand in for concrete objects or ideas. Signs include words (both written and spoken), gestures, architectural design, art works, musical notation and sounds, hair styles, dress, and any other range of the devices people use to connect with one another. Language is a representational system because it provides *something* to stand in for (to represent, to make present) *something else*. But it is not only representational. It also works as a system of reference because a word or other sign does not simply stand in for the thing, but also refers people to that thing. And it does more than this: language not only represents, refers or otherwise communicates aspects of the world. It also, according to most contemporary and many much earlier theorists, frames the world so that in particular ways the world becomes available or visible to us.

LANGUAGE AND LIMITS

In the sixteenth century the essayist Michel de Montaigne identified language as the generator of the limits set on our worldview. In his essay 'On the Cannibals' he writes about the tendency in all cultures to divide the world up into 'people like us' and 'barbarians', and to see 'barbarian' as the term for wild, dangerous and frightening outsiders. He goes on to point out that the word 'barbarian' is simply the Greek word for foreigner (1987: 2); it does not necessarily imply anything negative. And yet, 'every man calls barbarous anything he is not accustomed to; it is indeed the case that we have no other criterion of truth or right-reason than the example and form of the opinions and customs of our own country' (1987: 8). Those opinions and customs are embedded in and expressed in language. So, as Montaigne shows, the word 'barbarian' that in fact means simply 'not Greek' becomes a signal for everything 'outside', everything 'not like us'. It sets in place an idea of a world structured along lines of inclusion (us) and exclusion (barbarians); of that which is reasonable set against that which is reduced to an unassimilable otherness.

Montaigne's essay challenges this view. He recounts many examples of the barbarism of sixteenth-century Europe, and compares local behaviour and the quality of life in the so-called 'civilized' society with that of the people the Europeans called 'barbarous': people of what is now called Brazil. His essay reminds us that the idea that there might be a category of people called 'savage', 'barbarian' or 'primitive' is not a mirror of how things are, but a re-presentation of social and cultural attitudes – and especially of the idea that anyone not like me and mine must be vicious, crude, savage and repulsive. It is also, of course, an example of the capacity of language to fit us to the dominant local views of the world, and to (re)produce the world for us.

THE FUNCTIONS OF LANGUAGE

Ludwig Wittgenstein insists that readers should 'make a radical break with the idea that language always functions in one way, always serves the same purpose: to convey thoughts' (1958: §304). Rather, he argues, language serves many functions, and works in many ways. It is more than a medium for representation, more than a matter of conveying thoughts, or referring to an external reality. It is also a way of getting things done. Linguist J.L. Austin offers a similar perspective in his *How to do Things with Words*, where he identifies various types of 'utterances' (ways of making a statement) and their different functions. One of these utterances is the constative; **constative utterance** is the term for statements about the world (1975: 3). If you call home to say 'I'm on the bus, I'll be back soon,' or tell a child 'off to bed now, Santa will be here soon,' you are using language in a constative sense – describing a state of affairs that may or may not be true, and informing others about it. Constatives are instances of propositional knowledge: they offer a proposition that describes a state of reality that exists outside of the statement. It is also how most of us think about language and its uses in most situations: as a supplement to the world, a means of describing it and bringing it into presence through the substitution of a sign for the thing itself.

But Austin also describes a form of utterance that is not propositional – that does not offer a statement about the world. This is called the **performative utterance,** and it is an utterance that is more an act than a statement. It does not simply describe the state of affairs, but in fact brings it into being. He explains this concept by referring to the marriage ceremony: when the celebrant says, 'I now pronounce you man and wife', the listeners do not hear a constative utterance, that is, a description of what is going on. Rather, what the listeners hear is a statement that makes the marriage real – that brings the reality of the marriage into existence – and thus it is performative (1975: 5). This is an example of language that is not just representation; it is an action. It does not refer the reader or listener to a state of affairs by representing a reality outside language (the reality that two people are married), but actually creates that reality and, in the process of creating it, refers people to it.

Yet another use of language is as pure display – again, a non-representational form of communication. Poetry in particular fits this bill, especially when it is about form rather than content. An example is E.E. Cummings' poem 'r-p-o-p-h-e-s-s-a-g-r' [1923] that opens thus:

```
r-p-o-p-h-e-s-s-a-g-r
        who
a)s w(e loo) k
upnowgath
PPEGORHASS (1983: 1044)
```

This is, as the title and opening line hint, a poem about a grasshopper. How it works is another question, and one that people still wrestle over (is it a sonnet, though arranged oddly on a page? Is it an acrostic? Is it an attempt to represent the movement of a grasshopper gathering itself to leap?). Before I offer my own suggestions, look at an extract from another grasshopper poem, this one dating from the seventeenth century:

> The joys of earth and air are thine entire,
> That with thy feet and wings dost hop and fly;
> And, with thy poppy works, thou dost retire
> To thy carved acorn-bed to lie.
>
> Up with the day, the sun thou welcom'st then,
> Sport'st in the gilt-plats of his beams,
> And all these merry days mak'st merry men,
> Thyself, and melancholy streams. (Lovelace [1649] 1983: 334)

Each poem conveys something of the identity of grasshoppers – how they move, how they live, and what it might feel like to be a grasshopper. But they do it in very different ways. Lovelace's poem is didactic: it *tells* about the insect, and when we read it, it works according to the conventions of (seventeenth century) English poetry. The lines scan and rhyme, the imagery is vivid, and the tone is joyous and alive. It does not mirror or otherwise evoke the grasshopper, though: if you read the lines aloud, you will hear a jaunty but steady rhythm. The lines are set loosely in iambic pentameter (five pairs of syllables in unstressed/stressed pattern), the conventional form for poetry. But extra syllables slip in here and there to break the beat, introduce the movement that is called counterpoint, and lift the tone. Still, it is a poem about a grasshopper – one that describes it, but does not invoke it.

Cummings' poem, in contrast, is mimetic. It doesn't tell, but *shows* and in this is closer to resemblance than to the representative mode adopted by Lovelace. It is energetic, visual, and even visceral. The arrangement of the words and lines do not precisely resemble the movements of the insect, but it does work both figuratively and cognitively. The letters themselves hop about, leaping out of the words and out of order. The reader's brain must hop about too, juggling all the letters and phrases and words – apparent nonsense – to extract the sense that is this portrait of a grasshopper. Try to read those lines out loud: what you will probably hear yourself doing is fumbling, straining, stretching out sound – moving erratically; in short, your voice will 'do' a grasshopper.

MODES OF REPRESENTATION

So, although language is typically a vehicle for representation, it is not always representational. But let's pay attention now to how it is structured to work as a representational system. One approach taken to the function of language is that it is reflective. This approach is based on something very like the notion of resemblance, or mimesis, discussed in the previous chapter – that language simply reflects or resembles a meaning that exists in the world. This has its value, but as indicated in Austin's notion of the performative, not all utterances do reflect something that already exists in reality; some of them create reality. Furthermore, language cannot simply reflect or resemble real-world states; it can only frame and interpret them.

A second approach to language is the intentional one; this is based on the notion that any act of communication conveys precisely what the communicator intended. As Stuart Hall writes, 'it is the speaker, the author, who imposes his or her unique meaning on the world through language' (1997a: 25). There are problems with this approach; for one thing, speakers and authors can only communicate in the codes of language, and so are restricted in what they can say and how they can say it. It is not possible to 'impose a unique meaning ... through language', only to convey signs and texts that others will decode – perhaps producing a unique meaning, perhaps not. Anyone who has been involved in a discussion or an argument is likely to have had the experience of thinking themselves precise, only to hear their interlocutor make a very different sense of their utterance. All we can say in response is 'That is not what I meant'; but we cannot insist 'I'm right and you're wrong'. We cannot impose any meaning, let alone a unique one.

A third approach, and the one that will be the focus of this chapter, is the constructionist approach to language. This encompasses the notion that meaning is not reflected or imposed, but actually constructed, in the process of making representations. As Ludwig Wittgenstein pointed out nearly a century ago, *'The limits of my language* mean the limits of my world' (1922: §5.6). The novelist Walter Abish published a novel titled *Alphabetical Africa* that is a vivid demonstration of Wittgenstein's argument. In this novel a pair of jewel thieves race around Africa, accompanied by their moll Alva. But because of the arbitrary limits Abish has placed on each chapter, they can only go to certain places, meet certain people and perform certain acts. In the first chapter every word must begin with the letter A, leading to the awkward opening sentence:

> Ages ago, Alex, Allen and Alva arrived at Antibes, and Alva allowing all, allowing anyone, against Alex's admonition, against Allen's angry assertion: another African amusement ... anyhow, as all argued, an awesome African army assembled. (Abish 1974: 1)

The narrator (who is named 'author') chases the three characters across Africa through the course of 52 alphabetically organized chapters. It makes perfect, if somewhat contrived, sense. By the second chapter the letter B can be used, so the characters can 'be', or 'beat', or 'brood'. The novel continues thus, with the next letter in the alphabet available in each consecutive chapter. This means, for instance, that the narrator – who is trying to catch up with Alva and her sidekicks – cannot bring himself into the story until the ninth chapter, when the letter I becomes available. At this point it plainly becomes a first person novel, with the narrator announcing, 'Bit by bit I have assembled Africa' (1974: 21). But it is not until the twenty-third chapter that 'words' or the 'writer' can be expressed. By the middle of the book the whole alphabet is in use, and the full scope of the world can be represented. But then the narrative shrinks again, losing a letter each chapter as Africa crumbles back to (almost) nothing. By the final chapter only A is available again, and the whole thing winds down into an extended sigh:

> another avoidance another avocation another avid avowal another awareness another awakening another awesome age another axis another Alva another Alex another Allen another Alfred another Africa another alphabet. (1974: 152)

This tortuous and often very funny novel is itself a representation of the logic that the world and all we do in it can be present only to the extent that signs – the codes of signification – make them present. Certainly it is a ludicrously excessive example of the constructionist approach, but it does have considerable intellectual and practical valence, by *showing* (not just telling) the effects of language – understood here as a system of representation – on our access to reality.

MAKING IT WORK: SEMIOTICS AND REPRESENTATION

Stuart Hall writes of the constructionist approach to language and meaning-making that it incorporates two systems of representation:

> the *semiotic* approach is concerned with the *how* of representation, with how language produces meaning – what has been called its 'poetics'; whereas the *discursive* approach is more concerned with the *effects and consequences* of representation – its 'politics'. (1997b: 6)

The semiotic approach to representation depends on the notion that all uses of language begin with a (representational) sign. Semiotics, or 'the science of signs', is a discipline that develops knowledge about how individual objects take on meaning. Its official point of origin is the 1916 seminal book, *Course in General Linguistics* (*Cours de linguistique générale*), published by linguist Ferdinand de Saussure (1966). Saussure's approach is based on what was later called structuralism, since it held as a founding principle the notion that there are structural relationships between the fundamental elements in every society – though they will not necessarily be the same in different societies and different cultural contexts. His understanding of language is profoundly structuralist because it figures the world of communication as organized according to clear 'rules' – or structures – which govern the formation of all communication, and by extension govern other representational systems.

Saussure sets out the conventions of the discipline of semiology/semiotics: that language is a system of difference, built on an arrangement of signs. A sign, in Saussure's definition, is comprised of the **signifier** (the representative element: a word, image or sound) and the **signified** (the real-world element for which it stands). The connection between them, he writes, is not based on resemblance or intention, but on something entirely arbitrary – something cultural. 'The linguistic sign unites, not a thing and a name, but a concept and a sound-image' (Saussure 1966: 66–7). Unlike the system of resemblance (or iconicity), where there is a degree of similitude between signifier and signified, in semiotics the connection is purely arbitrary. For instance, under the system of resemblance the sign for 'stop' might be an image of a raised hand; this conveys 'stop' because it looks like someone putting their hand up in front of your face: a gesture likely to induce you to stop. But under semiotic representation, the sign for 'stop' might be a hexagon, or a red light: and their only connection to the idea of stopping is a cultural one. Such signifiers are what Saussure calls 'unmotivated' because each 'actually has no natural connection with the signified' (1966: 69), no necessary connection with the concept of stopping.

A second issue in Saussure's semiotics is that the meaning of a sign is not fixed: rather, a sign takes its meaning from other signs. A red light on the intersection of two streets means 'stop'; a red light on a weapons system might signify danger; a red light associated with images of attractive women might signify the presence of a brothel; a red light in the sky tells those who know that an aeroplane is flying overhead and that its port (left) side is visible. It is the context that determines the meaning of the light, in each case. But of course this is not all: we also have to contend with slips of the tongue and other oddities in the use of signs. On the news recently, for instance, the announcer declared: 'Next, the Native Title decision that has left fishermen reeling' (ABC 2007). A listener who took signs literally would have real trouble making sense of this. Are the fishermen reeling in shock because native title has awarded the control of fishing rights to indigenous Australians; are they reeling (dancing a reel) in joy because fishing rights have been settled in favour of commercial fishermen; or are they reeling in the fish now that they have control over the oceans? This is a silly example, but it does demonstrate the multiple meanings possible from any reading, and the importance first of the context and then of the rules of the code in which any sign is used.

Ideas about what a sign is, and can be, have been developed in several ways since Saussure's work, though they remain focused on signs and codes. C.S. Peirce offers what is perhaps the best-known definition, writing that a sign is:

> something which stands to somebody for something in some respect or capacity. It addresses somebody, that is, creates in the mind of that person an equivalent sign, or perhaps a more developed sign. ... The sign stands for something, its *object*. It stands for that object, not in all respects, but in reference to a sort of idea. (1955: 99)

This is a rather muddy definition for anyone not already familiar with the notion of sign; but at base is the notion that anything that seems to mean something to you is a sign. It may not have been generated intentionally by anyone; it may not have any relationship to actuality; but if you see it as expressing something, then it is indeed (for you) a sign. An example of this is the practice of necromancy, in which shamans read the entrails of slaughtered animals to foretell the future. To anyone not invested in the belief system that uses these practices, the 'signs' look entirely arbitrary or random – intestines, but not signs. But for those who do believe and have a code for the shapes and inter-relationships of the objects, they may speak of triumph in battle, the birth of a healthy child or the presence of a spy.

Let us take the idea of the sign a little further. We will stay with Peirce's notion that it is 'something which stands to somebody for something', and investigate the first 'something' in that phrase. For Peirce, that something may be an icon, an index or a symbol. All are signs, but they take different forms and perform different functions in the work of making meanings.

ICONS AND INDICES

An **icon** is a direct representation of something already known; a simulacrum for something in the real world. It is not the referent itself (i.e., the thing in the world) but it shares properties with that referent – it is 'like it' in a recognizable way. A portrait or photograph is typically iconic because it will be immediately recognizable 'as' the person that is the subject. Of course it is not in fact that person, but merely a sign, an icon, of him or her. Figure 2.1 (see over) is a photograph of the Victoria and Albert Museum's replica of Michelangelo's David. The original is, we assume, an excellent portrait of a young man – an iconic representation of that man, a close resemblance. It shares properties with that young man – the texture of his hair, the musculature of his shoulders, the angle of his cheekbones and so on. The historical narrative tells us that the portrait represents – refers viewers to – the figure of King David, an historical character from the Old Testament. We have no real idea of David's appearance so we don't actually know whether the portrait shares properties with the king, but we are prepared to accept Michelangelo's word for it, and to see the statue *as* David.

Of course no one who looks at a portrait of someone thinks they are seeing an actual physical person, let alone the Biblical king, but they will say 'That's David', meaning that the icon is sufficiently transparent so they know precisely whom the portrait represents. To make it all a bit messier, the image you see here is a photograph of a replica of an original statue of a living human being standing in for an ancient king. There is a very distant connection between the image and the actuality of the king – but nonetheless thanks to art history, Bible history and the popularization of this image, we can confidently look at it and give it a name – we can read its iconic value. It resembles its referent (the real young man in early sixteenth-century Florence); and it is connected to (the idea of) King David by a chain of other signs.

Figure 2.1   A *David* replica, V&A Museum (2006)

Unlike iconic signification, the **index** does not resemble its referent. Instead, it is influenced by the referent, and acted upon by it. Example of indices can be found everywhere: a bulb that lights up to signal that a lift has arrived at your floor is an index of its arrival; it does not resemble either a lift or an arrival, but the presence of the lift on the right floor acts upon the machinery, and this triggers the light that signals its presence. Lesions on the skin of a child similarly signal the presence of chickenpox, because though they do not resemble a disease, they are acted on by it and indicate its presence. And a weathercock is an index too, acting as a sign about how the wind is blowing. It does not work iconically (it doesn't in any way resemble the wind) but the action of the wind blowing on it causes it to swivel, and how it ends up indicates the direction of the wind. It signifies only because the wind acts on it.

SYMBOLIC SIGNS

Iconic and indexical representation are used by many living creatures: primates, for instance, readily recognize icons of food or drink, as many research projects have demonstrated. Many animals also recognize indexical signs: cattle might read a change in the wind pattern as a sign of an approaching storm; a dog might read the look on its master's face as an indication of displeasure. Symbolic meaning, though, seems to be pretty much entirely a property of human beings. Unlike icons and indexes, **symbols** are arbitrary, need have no connection whatsoever with their referent, and can be understood only by agreement among people – only because there are shared conventional meanings for that symbol. The meaning of a symbol depends not on resemblance (as with an icon) or association (as with an index), but by the relation between signs.

Figure 2.2 A bus route, Oxford (2006)

Figure 2.3   A point on the route, Oxford (2006)

To see more clearly the difference between the various modes of significa-tion, consider the difference between a map and a photograph of part of a city. A map will communicate something about that area, but only in symbolic mode. It is not iconic (i.e., it does not resemble the area) but is instead a highly abstracted representation of that area.

Figure 2.4 A point on the route, Oxford (2006)

Looking at it gives the viewer little sense of the texture of the place, or any idea at all of the topography or other actualities of the area. The (very crude) map depicted in Figure 2.2 shows that the bus on which the map is printed will take passengers from Grovelands, via the city centre, to Barton. A couple of points along the way are depicted in Figure 2.3 and 2.4. These three images all depict something about a particular locale; but they work in very different ways.

The first, the map, erases all information except the broadly directional: that the bus is passing through certain points and heading in certain compass directions. It is purely symbolic: nothing in the image looks like anything in the real world; it signifies only by virtue of a code understood by those familiar with bus schedules, and who can connect the lines and letters on the map to places they might wish to travel. The second image does something very different. It is of a point on the bus route, but it pays no attention whatsoever to the bus or the business of public transport. Its concern is with the old graves that remain in the town square; and it entirely ignores the comings and goings in the street beyond. Its concern is history; the present is caused to disappear. The third image is also of a part of the bus route; unlike the first (the map) it is not concerned with public transport or the direction of travel; unlike the second image (the graves) it is not concerned with the past, but with the here and now. Like the second, it is an icon: it contains objects, lines and tones that accord with how the world actually looks to us. It provides a different perspective on that part of the town, on that part of the bus route, and on ways of viewing the world.

Obviously, these images (signs) work according to different principles of signification, and communicate different content. The map is a symbol; it does not in any real sense resemble the area through which the bus will pass, though for those with knowledge of other signs (place names or routes) that provide it with a context, it makes sense. The photographs, on the other hand, actually resemble at least part of the space through which the mapped route passes. They will not help you work out which bus to take, or let you know where you are in relation to other points in the region, but they do give a taste of specific places in the area.

The point here is that symbols and icons are decidedly different beasts, as far as signification is concerned, and do very different tasks. However, this should not be taken to suggest that icons can never be symbols, or symbols indices. Peirce suggests that virtually all signs have features of the iconic, indexical and symbolic modes. For example, most signs will be partly iconic in that they denote by resembling their objects to some extent; partly indexical because they are really affected by their objects; and partly symbolic because they denote 'by virtue of a law', or code (Peirce 1955: 247–9).

MIXING IT UP

Sometimes a sign may obviously incorporate aspects of all three modes of signification. Let us return to that weathercock, which we left poised on the roof of someone's home. It acts as an indexical sign only while the link between itself and its referent is reliable. Suppose the homeowner couldn't tolerate the squeaking of the vane any more, and anchored it to prevent it from moving. Now we have a situation where it is still up there, and still signaling, but no longer indicating usefully. It has lost its role as an index, but can still be capable of making meanings under a different economy of signification.

It may, for instance, work as an icon: it resembles a rooster, albeit somewhat stylized, and so may remind viewers of chickens – with any number of implications. Maybe one viewer forgot to let the hens out before going off to work this morning and is guiltily reminded of this; another may decide vaguely to pick up some chicken for dinner tonight; another again may begin brooding about early mornings and noisy neighbours; yet another may mentally run through the lines of the famous William Carlos Williams poem, and wonder just what is so important about those white chickens.

The very same object-sign can work as a symbol, rather than meaning in and of itself (that is, neither standing in for poultry nor being acted on by the wind). Instead it can take on quite arbitrary meanings, based on the connection between itself and other signs in its context. It might, for instance, signify that the owner likes decorative features – particularly if there are other decorative features on the outside of the house; it might signify that a traditionalist lives in the house – particularly if the house is painted in heritage colours; it might, if there are objects on or near the house that are recognizable as religious symbols, be taken as having religious significance.

To explore this further, let's look at two warning signs. The first, a sign mounted in Hong Kong's airport (below), looks self-evident: it tells viewers that if there is a fire, they should run in the direction of the arrow. This sign is iconic because it resembles what is being told. There is a fire (and there is an

Figure 2.5 A warning sign, Hong Kong (2005)

indication of a fire); fire is dangerous (and so there is a person running away); and safety is implied (if you run in the direction signified: that is, away from the fire). There is no need for any linguistic representation; if you see it, no matter your level of literacy or the language(s) you speak, it communicates.

This sign is not only iconic, of course. The person ('person') does not in fact resemble any person you are likely to meet. The little lines behind the (quote unquote) person mean 'fire' only to those who know how to read the image. However, fire does flicker in a series of tongues of flame, and these marks could certainly be seen as individual flames, especially given the context: a public space, a multilingual space, the need to communicate with airport users in the most economical fashion. So certainly it is abstracted to a degree, and hence symbolic, but remains more in the domain of icon than a (Peircian) symbol.

Figure 2.6 A warning sign, London (2005)

The image (above), taken from Kensington Gardens in London, has a bit more going on. Like the previous sign, it is a public warning in a public venue, this time out of doors and near a lake. The warning triangle around the falling figure is one that draws attention to anyone accustomed to public signs and their codes, which are relatively similar around the world. It is, like the previous sign, somewhat abstracted: it takes both a leap of imagination and an awareness of context to make sense of the figure's base: the right arm and leg merge seamlessly with the ground, the lighter patches signal both the space between limbs and body, and also a pool of water. It is certainly iconic: its resemblance to a falling person is, we know culturally, a warning that you yourself might fall. But it also has indexical features. It warns of the danger of falling, and does so on a ground that has itself been acted on by the referent: it is deeply cracked – it has itself been damaged by the risks of which it warns – and now can be read double: as a sign that you might trip over the broken pavement, and that you might slip in a puddle of water.

THE POLITICS OF SIGNS

Both signs are symbolic too: they convey something ideological (or political) about their own context. Each figure is plainly male according to the rules of male/female coding in typical public signage. Neither has the long hair and skirt that typically signals 'female' – an icon we see, usually, on signs for public toilets or on road signs signalling pedestrians. In their assumption of the male as capable of standing in for human beings in general, each reinforces the masculinization of the public world. That is: for person, read man/male. 'Female' is invisible except when specifically needed, such as in the care of small boys at school crossings, or to support the interdiction against mixed-sex urination.

My suggestion here is that even the most innocent of public signs do not simply tell: that is, either indicate or act as icons of the everyday world. They also interpret that world – in these cases, according to the dominant public notions of value and according to the hierarchy of value, which still, thirty years after second wave feminism, sees women in a supplementary social position. In Vienna, Austria, this has changed after been critiqued by public commentators, as reported here:

> In place of the traditional 'Construction work ahead' symbol showing a man in trousers and helmet, they depicted a ponytailed woman wearing rugged-looking boots and a skirt. On 'Exit' signs, a running woman in skirt and high-heeled boots

replaced the traditional male stick figure. On a 'Beware the road is slippery' sign, the woman carried a little handbag. The prototypes, designed to encourage people to rethink gender biases, have provoked much criticism. ... 'This has nothing to do with emancipation,' wrote one reader [of Die Presse], Patricia Stocker. 'The traditional symbols of a skirt and high heels are ridiculous.' ... The road sign campaign in Vienna is part of a broader 'gender mainstreaming' strategy. But other public signs have drawn less controversy. Emblazoned on stickers in trams and buses is the silhouette of a man with a baby on his lap. ... And nappy-changing facilities now have signs involving men and women. (*Los Angeles Times* 2007: 13)

The point is not a simple one of the relative value of men versus women, but of the fact that even in the twenty-first century, people in positions of authority acknowledge the importance of representation in making the world that is available to individual human beings. Everything we see, hear or otherwise experience can be understood as a text capable of being analysed by applying the principles of signification.

MAKING IT WORK: DISCOURSE AND REPRESENTATION

The foregoing section outlined some of the ways in which scholars of semiotics undertand how representation works in language. But of course that is only one approach. Another, equally compelling perspective, is that of **discourse**, which Stuart Hall defines as follows:

> Discourses are ways of referring to or constructing knowledge about a particular topic of practice: a cluster (or formation) of ideas, images and practices, which provide ways of talking about, forms of knowledge and conduct associated with, a particular topic, social activity or institutional site in society. These discursive formations, as they are known, define what is and is not appropriate in our formulation of, and our practices in relation to, a particular subject or site of social activity. (1997b: 6)

Where semiotics focuses attention on the *structure* of language as a system, discourse pays attention to how, in different contexts, language is used in different ways that set up very specific relations and understandings. Each social space is likely to require a different use of language, or a different discourse. Think of how someone in their twenties dresses, moves and speaks when at a nightclub, at a job interview, in a university tutorial or when buying clothes. Each of these activities takes place in a different field, and each field has its own 'rules' for thinking, interacting and being, and its own expectations – usually met – for how one should dress, move and speak. Analysis of how representation functions in each of these fields illuminates how the everyday world not only works, but works to construct us, the humans who inhabit it.

Where Saussure initiated the study of semiotics, Michel Foucault is often seen as the seminal writer on discourse. He lays out his perspective in this quote from his *Power/Knowledge*:

> one's point of reference should not be to the great model of language (langue) and signs, but to that of war and battle. The history which bears and determines us has the form of a war rather than that of a language: relations of power not relations of meaning. ... Neither the dialetic, as logic of contradictions, nor semiotics, as the structure of communication, can account for the intrinsic intelligibility of conflicts. (1980: 114)

The point here is that everything we do is imbued with power and conflict, or conflict over power; hence the reference to war as both metaphor and actuality. Foucault dismisses semiotics as an analytical approach because he does not believe it sufficiently focuses attention on that struggle: meaning, for him, is not about the structure of representational systems, but about the production of regimes of truth. The two approaches share a common cause, though, in one of the fundamental principles that undergird each: the notion that language is a system of difference. For analysts who draw on approaches taken from discourse theory, this difference is perhaps most evident in what is called 'binary oppositions'.

THE LOGIC OF BINARY OPPOSITION

Binary logic is considered, especially by structuralist theorists, to be the fundamental organizing mode of human societies and human thought. It is based on the observation that the world is typically (at least for the inheritors of Greek philosophical thought) ordered around pairs of oppositional elements or ideas. These two items are connected logically or practically, and yet are always in opposition to each other: in other words, a term defines itself both against and in terms of its other (Lacan 1977a: 208). The word 'presence', for example, is related to 'absence' by opposition; 'man' is similarly related to 'woman', and 'nature' to 'culture'. This may sound rather like the game of associations often played in school or with therapists, but rather more is involved here. For instance, in associative thinking, the word 'black' might evoke the response 'white', or 'cat', or 'magic', or 'sun'. In binary thinking, 'black' can only evoke 'white'. And, theorists go on to point out, in binary thinking one half of the pair is always dominant. There is, in fact, an order (a structure) in Western thought that doesn't just set elements in pairs, but always sees each pair connected to other pairs in a chain of consequence. It could be set out something like this:

God	Creation
Man	Woman
Culture	Nature
Reason	Emotion
Public	Private
Order	Chaos
Presence	Absence

The connections go both horizontally and vertically: the horizontal plane is the relationship of opposition and dominance, and the vertical plane is the relationship of connection and confirmation. For instance, man is dominant over woman because man has presence (a phallus), is committed to reason and the public domain, is organized and ordered, and represents 'culture' rather than the chaotic, emotional, state-of-nature, *lacking* domain that can be summed up in 'woman'. Simone de Beauvoir, Germaine Greer and Elizabeth Grosz (among many others) have shown how this structure of thinking has served to keep women from taking up a place as full social **subjects**; Edward Said, Gayatri Spivak and Homi Bhabha (also among many others) have shown how this same binary logic enabled the domination and abuse of colonized people by the European invaders/settlers. This can happen because binary oppositions may be framed in terms of two related, differentiated words, but in fact are not about the word; rather, they are about what Elizabeth Grosz (2005) calls 'two tendencies or impulses, only one of which is the ground of the other'. A word is only a representation – a substitute for – an attitude, in this case. Changing the word in the binary pair will not change their relative position, or the way they are structured as each other's opposite, because the difference between them is one of relation – here, relations of power – not one of nominology or logic.

Binary logic depends firstly on everyone – both those in power and those being dominated – believing that it is a true and valid way to understand the world, and then on the dominant having the force, or physical power, to ensure that the dominated stay in their place. This means it is an unstable system, liable at any moment to be disrupted by revolutionary force, and the relations of power inverted. It is unstable too because the two elements are never independent of one another: 'culture' may be the valued half of the binary, but it is itself only because there is 'nature' to define it by not being it, by being instead 'its absence, its lack, the dialectical confirmation of its identity' (Butler 1990: 44). As soon as a woman, for instance, insists on knowing why 'reason' is part of the chain of 'man', and hence superior to 'emotion' (which is part of the chain of 'woman') and why 'man' is necessarily connected to 'reason' and not to 'emotion', the possibility of establishing a secure and unchangeable meaning breaks down. Perhaps men could respond that 'man' is not 'emotional'; and this might be valid, or once have been valid, if by emotional we mean that men do not sob weepy movies, or cluck over babies (though of course many men do just this). But emotion includes fits of temper, deep anxiety, depression, joy – and men are no less subject to these than are women. So the disconnect between 'man' and 'emotion' that is built into that system of binary opposition sketched out above can't be supported by the evidence of actual human behaviour; and as soon as a tremble of uncertainty is set up in that chain of binary oppositions, the whole thing threatens to fall apart.

The problem is not one of difference per se, but of the meaning of those perceived differences. Michel Foucault writes:

> For a thing to be different, it must first no longer be the same; and it is on this negative basis, above the shadowy part that delimits the same, that contrary predicates are then articulated. (1970: 183–4)

First we need to recognize that there is a process by which certain qualities become framed as difference, rather than sameness – for instance, by tracing the process by which women are considered not-men. In fact, of course, there are very few actual differences between women and men, but this sameness is hidden, Foucault writes, in the shadow necessary to make the system of power relations function.

Jacques Derrida has given considerable attention to the issue of binary oppositions, differences and sameness, and he argues that since language, based as it is on difference, has driven a wedge between the two sides of the binary, we need a third term in which both can participate. This term is found in the 'shadowy part': he names it *différance*, a term that is both sameness (it is *similar to* 'difference') and difference (it is *not identical* with 'difference'). The word sounds like 'difference' (i.e., the basis of binary oppositions) but looks misspelt (Derrida 1968: 3). In this way it draws attention to its own difference from 'difference' as a way of pointing out the arbitrary nature of meaning-making, and the impossibility of pinning down meaning – and hence relations of power – in any final way. Just as men and women are same-if-different – as are all pairs in the binary logic – so too *différance* accommodates both sides of the equation. Acknowledging the sameness-in-difference that is the condition of every pair of binary opposites means the barriers between the two elements can be dissolved, the dependence of each element on the other can be made evident, and the power relations changed.

The point is that meaning-making has what Foucault calls a 'violent, bloody and lethal character'; and for him, at least, it is not understood through semiotics which merely reduce it to 'the calm Platonic form of language and dialogue' (Foucault 1980: 115). Representational systems are, from this perspective, first and foremost about politics, or the relations of power between individuals and groups.

DEFERRAL AND DIFFERENCE

Derrida's neologism also points out another feature of language, understood as a representational system: it is not only structured in terms of difference; it is also about deferral. Meaning cannot be finalized; it is always deferred, its end point held over from utterance to utterance, context to context. It never actually delivers, but only defers, presence (Derrida 1968: 9). Let's go back to our pairs of opposites. We know already from the information in the section above on semiotics that the symbolic representation is arbitrary, and based on difference. The word 'I' means 'I' because its referent (me) is not 'you', or 'ewe'. Another term could just as easily have been selected to name the element we call 'I', without doing any damage to the concept; (or, as Shakespeare put it, 'that which we call a rose by any other name would smell as sweet' *Romeo and Juliet*, II, ii, 1–2).

This arbitrary connection between the sign and its signified, or the representation and its referent, means that however stable a meaning might appear to be, it only works in a given context (as we saw above); it only works momentarily; and it only works as long as all parties to the communication share an understanding not only of the code, but also of the logic – the politics – that lie behind the code. What is shown in the discursive approach to analysis of representation is the terms of that code. It shows how texts make their meanings, on what their 'truths' are based, what are the hidden or expressed assumptions, what traits are valued and what traits are dismissed. Derrida's *différance* provides the philosophical framework for arguments that show each element in a binary is connected to its other not actually by an oppositional relation – not just by difference – but by interdependence. Man is man because he is not woman; and yet in all but a very few empirical characteristics, man and woman are identical. We have virtually identical DNA, body shape, physiological and neurological processes, and responses to the physical environment. The *meaning* of 'man' qua 'man' can be sustained only when the actualities of the situation are ignored. That same meaning can be challenged: not by saying, for instance, woman should be dominant over man, but by showing the samenesses and the interdependencies between man and woman.

To explain further the ways in which the discursive approach can be used to indicate how a 'truth' is produced in a text, and the extent to which binary oppositions can be both invoked and pulled apart, let us examine the image embedded below.

This is a photograph taken in Copenhagen of an artwork located in a park, and invaded by a passerby. The artwork itself mirrors a particular view of Western society: two people, of opposite gender, together, taking their ease in the sun. But are they indeed of opposite gender? The sculpture on the left of the photograph seems to be a representation of a man – the broad shoulders, strong jawline, confident posture and hint of male genitalia support this: it is a man, taking his ease, in the sun. But is he indeed taking his ease – and is the artwork depicting someone enjoying sunshine? His arms are tensely folded, his shoulders raised, his feet flexed, his head tilted back in what could as easily be pain as comfort. The pleasure/pain binary is thus put under pressure.

What of the male/female binary? The second sculpted figure may well be a woman: the smaller size, the delicacy of the facial features, the more con-strained posture and the expectation that where you have male, the accom-panying element will be female, all support this. But this figure is sexually ambiguous: there are no obvious breasts; there is a hint of a penis; the shoul-ders are broad, as they are on the first figure.

And beyond this, the question of whether they are in fact 'together' is put in doubt. Viewers are led to assume this, since two strangers would be unlikely to sit close together on the same bench. Their proximity implies

Figure 2.7 © Paul Travers 2006

familiarity – but they do not touch, they do not lean towards each other, they do not even gesture towards eye contact. Nor do they look particularly happy. The pleasure of a couple taking in the sun is undermined as much as it is set up, and the 'truth' of what it means to be together in the world is critically engaged by this piece.

What, then of the third character, the human? Here we could see other binaries – sentient/non-sentient, human/product, the elegance of art versus the sloppiness of the everyday; and so on. Yet the three characters are similar in size, shape and similar in posture. All three share a physical location, and what we can assume is a similar yearning for sun and pleasure, but all are bleak in appearance. The promise of the park – the space where nature meets culture – is not achieved. The photograph is structured ostensibly in terms of binary oppositions, but as fast as we identify each binary, the refusal of any sustainable opposition is also identified. It demonstrates throughout the way in which, for every binary opposition, the two elements will always intertwine with each other, and rely on each other; and the social truths initially proposed by the binary logic will come to be seen as only the artefacts of a system of power and representation.

CONCLUSION

'Words have usages, it is said, rather than essential meanings, and a careful analysis of their various usages is likely to be more fruitful than a concentration of attention on the common element in these usages, which may be of only etymological significance' (Birch 1971: 13). It is important to bear this in mind, in any consideration of language and/as representation: all instances of signification are based on something arbitrary, and are empty of meaning as such, but full of potential. And while there is nothing natural or necessary about how signifying systems are organized, there is a great deal that is political or 'interested' about them.

3 Representation and the subject/ the subject of representation

The previous chapters have pointed out the gap between reality and representation, and the difficulty in succeeding in what the concept's name suggests it can do: to re-present; to make present again. This chapter introduces the idea of the subject, which is to say *people*: me, you, and everyone else in the world. This, it could be assumed, drags the question of reality and presence back into the equation. Surely if there is one real thing, it is an individual human existence? Each of us has an empirical being – we can be measured and recorded, our existence can be tested and our life compassed. We don't have to be *represented*: we simply *are present* in a time and place, each one of us a discrete, particular individual in a world of other particular individuals.

Like pretty well every other answer to any question about representation, this question of the real presence of individuals can only be answered yes, and no. Yes, each of us certainly is an empirical individual; we *are*. But each of us is also present in the world as a mediated individual. We may be real, but we are also social, and hence socialized, which means the way we understand ourselves and others, and the way we engage with ourselves and others, is always framed by cultural knowledges and imperatives – by modes of representation, not by actuality.

In the twentieth and twenty-first centuries, the media of representation have contributed to this ambiguity about what constitutes a self. The digital environment has enabled new modes of existence and identity, new ways of representing oneself and being represented. Facebook, 'a social utility that connects you with the people around you' (splash page, http://www.facebook.com); MySpace, 'a space for friends' (splash page, http://www.myspace.com/); Second Life, 'a 3D online world imagined and created by its residents' (splash page, http://secondlife.com/): these sites and others like them allow individuals to represent, or indeed construct, their identity in purely digital form, and enable the existence of 'people' who are in fact only pixels and data sets, born of the imagination of their creators and the software programs used to produce them.

But whether digital or material, I suggest, human subjects *become* within, and inhabit, a world that is simultaneously real and representational. For instance, although the actuality of the digital world means people can do anything at all, they tend to do in their avatar form pretty much what they do in the 'real world' – they have jobs, they buy commodities, they flirt and date. Anything goes, but what in fact occurs is what fits the social context and the representational frameworks that individuals understand, and within which they understand themselves (Boss 2007). We have physical sensation; we are thinking and speaking individuals; we interact with others and the world; yet we do so only according to fairly clear patterns and 'rules'.

In this chapter I discuss the main ways in which theorists have understood the emergence of the thinking, speaking, mediated human from the bundle of undifferentiated sensations that is a human infant. This brings in some very contemporary analysis of that which lies outside the domain of representation: those parts of consciousness that seem to pertain to the physiological processes of the body, rather than to the representational domain of the social world. In short, I attempt to write across and between two very different worlds: that of language/the social/representation, and that of whatever lies beyond, or outside articulation, what cannot be understood: the real/nature/sensation.

CHICKENS AND EGGS

In the previous chapter I raised the question of whether we use language and representation, or it uses us: what is the point of origin for meaning? This is a bit like the chicken-and-egg question: which comes first? Obviously human beings in their physical integrity came first; but even in very early human communities, researchers have been finding, there is evidence of representational activity. We have long known about cave paintings, of course, and have used them to date the presence of prehistoric communities; but very early humans, and even Neanderthals, seem to have made and worn ornaments, and to have taken care of the remains of their dead. This suggests they had characteristics much closer to that of modern humans than of animals: the ability to think abstractly, and to make representations. In answer to the chicken-and-egg question, then, perhaps all we can say is that as humans emerge in history, so too does representation; and that changes in human cultures come about because of, or alongside, changes in systems and logics of representation. It is not that one precedes the other; rather, humans are in representation, and representation is in humans.

This is how we can understand it when thinking about the great mass called 'human beings'. But when it comes to one individual, someone called 'me', there does seem to be more pressure brought from the processes of representation onto the individual than vice versa. Philosophy has, throughout history, attempted to understand this relationship, and how individuals, born into the world as undifferentiated little bundles, become speaking, identifying and representing human beings.

LANGUAGE AND THE SELF

One perspective on how a person becomes a person – a recognized member of the human community – is based on language, and the acquisition of language. We identify things because they are named. The moment someone is born, we give them a name. The moment we discover a comet, or a movement of molecules, or a new flower, we give it a name. The world exists for us because we have language; because we pin it down by representation. Indeed, according to Roland Barthes, this is how we manage the enormity of the universe: 'What I can name cannot really prick me' (1981: 51). We are not just naming-machines, though; as M.D. Tschaepe writes, 'one does not first emerge within the world as a language user, but rather, as a body that perceives' (2003: 68).

I will come back to the issue of embodiment below, and for now focus on the fact that human beings are born into a world of language; we acquire language, or the capacity to use it; and we are recognized as fellow language-users by other members of our community. It is this, many theorists have argued, that gives us our social identity. This (very **logocentric**) view emerges from the work first carried out by Sigmund Freud, and then developed by Jacques Lacan. It suggests that an individual's identity is a very tenuous thing. Rather than something we are born with, it is something we develop; and something we could, therefore, lose. Indeed, the very basis of subjectivity, for Lacan, is loss or lack: we become ourselves by losing ourselves.

Let me explain this more fully. An infant is born without language and without the capacity to differentiate between any of the signs in her vicinity. Nothing 'means'; everything just 'is'. She has physical awareness, of course, and will respond to hunger or pain, but cannot see difference. She can communicate only through unintelligible vocalizations – like the infant in Figure 3.1 (see over) – not by making representations. She can perceive, but only in terms of colour and movement. That is to say, her perception is awareness, but not vision: she is living in a world that is only semiosis, not signification, and she is not yet able to distinguish object from object.

Gradually, as the infant's brain starts to firm up, distinctions will become evident: she will first be able to identify a face from all the blur of signs before her; and then, out of all possible faces she will identify her mother's face.

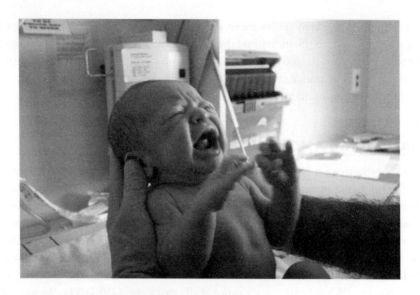

Figure 3.1 and 3.2 © James Webb 2005

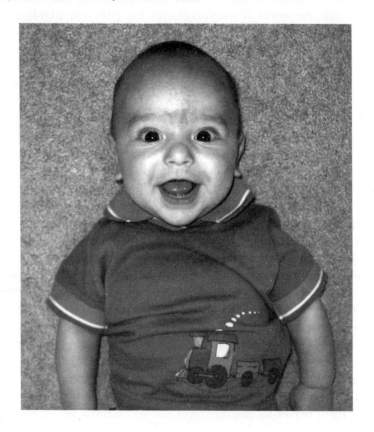

Now things are starting to become meanings: she is no longer restricted to basic physiological sensation, but attaches sense to what is around her. She still can't make representations, but is beginning to understand difference. Her own hand, for example, changes from being just a part of her environment, to something she finds she can move at will, to something that, if moved in a particular way, means 'goodbye'.

Despite these developing understandings she is not yet human, in that she is not yet admitted to the community of human beings; for instance, she is not considered capable enough to be allowed to vote or enter into commercial contracts. She is in what philosophers call the **chora**: a kind of third space or, in Derrida's interpretation of Plato, a 'halfway place', or 'half place' (Derrida 1995a: 116). She is no longer a blob of cells, but not yet one of us. And for her too, the world is a chora: no longer a mass of undifferentiated signs, but not yet the organized and knowable world of the full symbolic subject.

THE MIRROR PHASE

She approaches this identity of symbolic subject by the age of about eighteen months, the age when most babies understand that the image they see in a mirror is themselves, and not another baby, or just a bit of colour and movement. Lacan identified this, the **mirror phase**, as central to the whole process of becoming human; and certainly it makes sense for people in the Western tradition, based as it is on difference. Up to this stage, the baby has begun to understand that there are different things, and differences between things: her own mother is not the same as other mothers, or as the family cat, or as her teddy bear. One blanket might seem different, to her, from all other blankets, and be the one she carries around everywhere. Food has different tastes and textures, some she likes and some she rejects.

So the world is becoming a place of signs that differ from one another, and have meanings. But as Lacan suggests, she herself is not yet fully cut out from the world of signs, and things: she does not yet understand that everything else in the world is not-her; she has not yet discovered the logic of distance, difference and deferral.

This is what comes to her at the mirror phase. When she looks in the mirror and first realizes 'That's me!' she not only discovers herself, someone or something utterly different from everything else, and therefore a particular person, but she also discovers lack (see over). This series of photographs shows the small girl coming to recognize her image in the glass, with its related gain and loss. The very act of recognizing her image in the glass requires a distancing ('That's me, over there') and necessarily produces a

Figure 3.3 The 'mirror phase'

split in her sense of self – in her subjectivity (Lacan 1977a: 188). From then on she will know herself *as* herself – me and only me, different from everyone and everything else. As Deleuze puts it:

> how do I know I am me, and not you? Because I perceive a difference; because the things I conceive, imagine, remember, are mine and not yours; because I compare 'me' with 'you', and come up with a difference, with a space between us. (1994: 137–8)

But this moment of coming to know myself as myself is thus also the moment of discovering lack. The movement from curiosity, to anxiety, to pleasure signals this process. I am me, but not just me – I am divided between myself as I experience 'me', and the representations I make of that 'me'. I see myself in a mirror, and it is me and not me. I call myself 'me' in conversation, and in the act of doing so I separate that 'me', the one spoken of, from 'I', the speaking self. In achieving my symbolic and divided self, I lose the connectedness of me.

Figure 3.4 © Paul Travers 2006

A second loss is that of full connection with all the things of the world. As an infant there is no distinction between myself and everything I experience. But now, as a symbolic subject, I find myself isolated from everything else, and from other people. There is no way of achieving that initial sense of oneness once we move under the logic of representation. Instead, we slide, back and forth, between the experienced and the represented self, between the self and the world, between the body and the image. Just as the meaning of language is based on difference and is endlessly deferred, so too the individual subject of and in representation is based on difference, and can never achieve fullness: the 'me' is always deferred. As novelist John Updike wrote, 'Not only are selves conditional, but they die. Each day, we wake slightly altered, and the person we were yesterday is dead' (1989: 211).

THE FRACTURED SELF

A term often used to explain this is 'decentring'. We are 'decentred subjects' because we lack a centre – we have no fixed sense or locus of self. If we were constantly aware of this lack, it would be very difficult to function in any way as a social being. But, having given us the lack, representation then moves in to stabilize our identity by putting itself in the place of the absent 'reality', making it seem 'really there' (Butler 1990: 43), providing us with a sense of presence and hence security. It gives us the tools to name and frame ourselves as concrete and coherent identities, and to find a position from which to represent ourselves; thus to move from being objects (that which is spoken about) to being subjects (that which speaks). We develop a fiction of an integrated self by becoming part of the social world – people able to vote and enter into commercial contracts. And this we do by taking up a position in what Lacan calls the **Symbolic order** (1977b: 65). This is part of the structure of society, that unwritten set of cultural rules organized by discourses of what is right and proper, and of how things should be. It is the domain, as it were, of representation.

How we enter it is a topic of debate among scholars. For Foucault, it is largely through being recorded in public documents, such as birth certificates, that both announce our identity and authorize it. For Louis Althusser, it is the effect of ideology that '**interpellates**' us – or names us within a system, or order ('inter' – within; 'appellation' – naming). His example goes like this: someone knocks at the door. I say, 'Is it you?' and when they say 'Yes' and I open the door, there you are (1994: 129-30). The one named 'you' has identified himself or herself as a distinct individual, cut out of the herd of possible 'yous'. Althusser explains further: 'Ideology is a "representation" of the Imaginary Relationship of Individuals to their Real conditions of existence' (1994: 123). The suggestion is that if the reality is too awful, ideology will reframe it so you can cope, or feel you can cope. This is a 'real' thing in itself, of course, however imaginary might be the relations it constructs. As Althusser goes on to point out, 'Ideology has a material existence' (1994: 125) – material in that it produces us, constitutes us, calls us into being for particular purposes, and 'enlists' us into systems of belief and hence of practice.

What does this mean, in effect? For me, it means I am interpellated as an academic. I know this because it says so on my contract of employment, because people refer to me as an academic, and because I do academic work. It means too that I am interpellated, or named, 'mother'. I know this is true because it says so on my children's birth certificates, and in letters sent to me by people I call my children. When I hear someone call 'Mum' I turn around.

I believe I am a mother, and (in at least some ways) I behave like a mother. Both these identities are objectively real in that there is evidence to support them; both work mainly in the telling – the process of naming that makes me 'me'.

MAKING IT REAL

This may seem just too tricksy; after all, what could be more straightforward than 'me'? There may indeed be philosophical or linguistic ideosyncracies, but experientially, surely we always know who we are and what we mean? Fair enough: within limits. It is true that the idea of the divided self is a fairly new one. It is, in part, a product of Enlightenment thought which, as we saw in Chapter 1, posited the cool, detached and rational observer, in the place of the experiencing and believing subject. Of course, people have always experienced a tension between themselves and others: ancient writings such as the *Ramayana* or the *Psalms*, and more recent ones like Shakespeare's *Hamlet* or *Macbeth*, show how difficult it has always been for people to understand the space between themselves and the world, or what they should do in that space. In the sixteenth century, Montaigne wrote lines that sound as though they were written by Jacques Lacan: 'I do not find myself in the place where I look; and I find myself more by chance encounter than by searching my judgement' (cited in Judovitz 1988: 11). This is a radical shift from the classical notion of knowing oneself, or the Enlightenment notion of calm reason.

The notion of the subject as I have described it above ushers in a new tension, a sense of infinite deferral, of infinite impossibility that we can know ourselves or be known. Frank Ankersmit locates this change in the nineteenth century:

> it was Romanticism that postulated a self which could never completely and fully realize itself in its social roles, for which its social manifestation was always a painful truncation of the self and a vexing violation of our authenticity. For what we are could never be made visible, not even to ourselves in our public presentation of ourselves. (2003: 325)

This is based in part on the way society was organized before the modern era, before the period of specialization and the drawing of a clear distinction between public and private life. The rise of schools and factories, for instance, took education and production away from the family home and/or the village. New conceptions of who counted, and as what sort of a person, as well as new pressures and demands on individuals, families and small communities broke the older ways of being where there was, at least to some extent, a 'place for everyone and everyone in his place'. Now there were new places and new ways of being in them; yet along with the discourses of freedom were new practices of oppression and confinement.

The shifts in how society was organized and its meanings framed, as well as the shifts in how and what people were understood to be, brought increasing pressures on the sense of individuality and subjectivity. It is also in this period that the negative effects of society came under scientific scrutiny, along with 'new' diseases (associated with factory conditions and crowded, unhygienic cities) and 'new' social problems (levels of suicide, family breakdown and violence).

THE LOGIC OF PRONOUNS

Of course none of these – with the possible exception of factory conditions – were really new. They were just being represented in a new way, as an effect of what Foucault would call a new **episteme**. Episteme is his term for periods of history organized around specific world views, or specific representational systems. Each period has its own way of framing the world and making truths, and its own way of making people into subjects. The modern episteme is marked, as I noted above, by difference and deferral, and hence by individuation on the part of individuals, and by lack. This is not universal though. In other cultures in this period, different understandings obtain, and the way to become and remain a subject likewise differs.

For example, a central concept of subjectivity in Africa is committed to the principle of **ubuntu**, a humanistic ideal that can be loosely translated as, 'a human being is only human in relation to other humans'. Consequently, according to writer and activist Mbulelo Mzamane, 'the true measure of our humanity is whether we can relate to and honour other humans' (2001). This, which locates our very being in community, is in sharp contrast to the contemporary Western representation of humanity, directed as it is at the quest for individual self-fulfilment and individual lack. The Western tradition finds no content to the pronoun 'we': Emile Benveniste writes that 'we', or any other personal pronoun, is an impossible term. Pronouns, he insists, only make sense in relation to 'conjunctions of past usage(s) with present appropriation' (1971: 291), and so they are instances of discourse: they do not represent something actually there. There is no 'we'; and only because someone says it is there, an 'I'. Perhaps no one took this logic quite as far as Samuel Beckett, whose work consistently brings into question the speaking subject, the status of the 'I', or the idea that the individual either has any stable place in the world, or can be differentiated from other individuals. Rather, each person is simply and sadly the product of culture and representation.

But while the Western tradition struggles to find meaning in the personal pronoun, other cultures find at least the first person plural, 'we', packed with content. In Pacific cultures, for instance, identity is found not in 'I' but in 'we'. Subjects are subjects because they belong to extended families and community networks. This is not to say that there is no notion of individual subjectivity, but at least under the traditional way of being and knowing, a person becomes a person because they have a network of connections, and they are not made in isolation by the chilly hand of representation. Pacific 'becoming' is as one of many, rather than as the isolated individual of Western culture. And this 'becoming' provides very different opportunities, and places very different limits, on individuals than might have happened in a different culture, with different language, values and systems of representation.

LINGUISTIC FRAMES

A short story by Primo Levi deals with this problematic, and the centrality of language in forming the possibilities of being. It opens by describing a star in an enormous, hot universe very far away. Then the narrator interrupts the story to worry about the capacity of language to deliver us the world and our place in it:

> We have written 'very far,' 'big,' 'hot,' 'enormous': Australia is very far, an elephant is big and a house is bigger, this morning I had a hot bath, Everest is enormous. It's clear than something in our lexicon isn't working. ... For a discussion of stars our language is inadequate and seems laughable, as if someone were trying to plow with a feather. It's a language that was born with us, suitable for describing objects more or less as large and as long-lasting as we are; it has our dimensions, it's human. It doesn't go beyond what our senses tell us. Until two or three hundred years ago, small meant the scabies mite; there was nothing smaller, nor, as a result, was there an adjective to describe it. (2007: 73)

The limits of our being, for Levi, are framed by our language, or our capacity to make representations of what is around us. What else might we be or become, given a different representational system? How else might we live with each other and with our world?

One way of answering this question is to look at representational systems and frameworks that are not our own, to see how else it might be done. Paul Collis, a representative of an indigenous Australian community, provided an example by describing what earthquakes mean to his community (Collis 2007). Those phenomena are perceived, and represented, as the land being distressed. Since 'the land is my mother', he said, the right response to an earthquake is to get together with the family, seek reassurance, and attempt to make things right.

The Western scientific view, of course, takes a very different perspective. It uses systems of measurement, observation and analysis to understand the structure of the earth, determine where the fault lines run, attempt first to predict where the next quake might emerge, and then to ameliorate its effects by scientific and governmental intervention.

Neither perspective is any more 'true' than the other. The land is indeed distressed: it has experienced a major upheaval in its very structure. The land is indeed also 'faulty' – it has weak points in its structure. But the two perspectives use very different forms of language and epistemological frameworks to make sense of what is going on, and work from very different philosophical bases. The Western epistemological framework is based on an ideology of knowledge and *disconnection* – the 'neutral distance' between observer and observed. The indigenous Australian epistemological framework is based on knowledge and *connection* – the intimate intertwining of the observer and observed. In the scientific view, the land 'goes wrong' because it 'has a fault'; in the indigenous view the land shakes because it is 'distressed': because the land is suffering. Although both traditions use systems of close observation and then representation to gather and communicate knowledge and understanding, they come at it from different angles and, inevitably, achieve different findings. In the scientific view, there is no real relational aspect between people and the earth. We are detached from it; it is simply the object being observed; and any remedial action is tied to mechanical interventions. But in the indigenous view we cannot stand outside or be detached from it: we are all born into, and intimately rely on, the crust of the earth, and relational actions are the appropriate responses.

Again, one view is not more correct than another, or better than another. Each is simply the product of a particular culture, and is based on verifiable knowledges and on use for purpose in particular contexts. In the context of a heavily populated world and densely populated urban environments, it is necessary to understand the physical and mechanical aspects of earthquakes; in a hunter-gatherer community with small populations and low buildings, a more useful framework is connection with the earth-as-mother. The same event is, therefore, represented according to impossibly different terms, with very different implications for how members of each community understand their own identity and their place in the world. And the implications are limited – or delimited – by the terms of representation that obtain in each culture.

BEING IN THE WORLD

The Western view, as I have detailed it above, describes how an individual human moves from being a baby, the object of sensation, to being an adult and the subject of perception. But this should not be taken as suggesting that sensation disappears as a mode of being once someone moves into the symbolic world that is the social order. Representation cannot contain everything. As Maurice Merleau-Ponty writes:

> There is a perpetual uneasiness in the state of being conscious. At the moment I perceive a thing, I feel that it was there before me, outside my field of vision. There is an infinite horizon of things to grasp surrounding the small number of things which I can grasp in fact. (1964: 28)

If we understand that the world is, for us, limited by cultural and linguistic frames, then we must understand too that the things not contained within those frames don't just disappear, or cease to exist. They exist elsewhere, and from time to time we will catch a glimpse of something unknown, out of the corner of the eye. This is a troubling experience, approaching the uncanny. Merleau-Ponty explains it here:

> An old jacket lying on a chair will be a riddle if I take it just as it offers itself to me. There it is, blind and limited; it does not know what it is; it is content to occupy that bit of space – but it does so in a way I never could. It does not run in all directions like a consciousness; it remains solidly what it is; it is in itself. (1964: 29)

In every reminder that *mine* is not the only way of being, or the only way of perceiving, is a threat to my existence, based as it is on the principles of difference and deferral. People live as though it were a natural thing to do; as though it could be done without thought; as though it were just a matter of getting on with things. But we are not jackets that do not know what they are; we are tricky, troubled and troubling creatures of representation, at once limited by our own frames, and at the same time offered alluring hints that things could be other than they seem to be; that there is more to the world than me and my perceptual frames.

The issue here is that while we become subjects within a world of language and representation – the ephemeral world of thought – we are still living embedded in a world of objects and of other living forms. For Merleau-Ponty (1968: 137), the subject exists as a part of the whole world it perceives: both thought and object, both known and not known; both perceived and felt. This means that just as our identity is always deferred – we never achieve a fullness or a wholeness – so too our status as subject is only just held back from being object. We exist in the world as 'ourselves' because language and representation call us into being, and presence; but they call everything else into presence too.

What makes human beings different from jackets or trees? One answer is that a jacket or a tree is pure matter; we humans are both matter and mind.

The mind is the perceiving, subject part of the self; the body is the perceived, object part of the self. The mind speaks; the body is silent. This is the basis of René Descartes' famous dictum, *cogito, ergo sum* [I think, therefore I am]. But this simply defers the answer to the question. Descartes' *cogito* locates our identity – our whole sense of self – in the mind and in the capacity of the brain to perceive, conceptualize and, in short, to represent. The body is seen as simply the shell in which the true person (the thinking self) lives. But there is a measurable relationship between the feeling body and the perceiving mind, and the cogito alone does not explain how this relationship can function.

COGITO, ERGO SUM?

Descartes has attracted considerable criticism in the past centuries for this dualist approach to the nature of *human* being. One critic, William James, argues that the body is 'the storm centre, the origin of co-ordinates, the constant place of stress in all that experience-train. Everything circles around it and is felt from its point of view' (1967: 284). Which sounds rather like: *I feel, therefore I am*. James' contemporary Friedrich Nietzsche directly challenged Descartes. 'It is merely a formulation of our grammatical habits,' he wrote, 'that there must always be something that thinks when there is thinking' (1968: §276, 309, 367): in other words, it is not necessarily 'me' thinking, and therefore it is not necessarily true, in those terms, that I am. Martin Heidegger continued in this line; he reversed Descartes' phrase, suggesting it makes better sense if set as *sum, ergo cogito*, or, *I am, therefore I think* (Heidegger 1949). His point was that existence is *Being*-in-the-world, not *Thinking*-in-the-world, and wanted to bring attention to the fact that we are physical, material creatures, not the product of ideas. Like Heidegger, Arthur Schopenhauer insists that the starting point for perception of the world is the individual's own body, and so it is also the very foundation of representation (1969: Book 1, §6). And Maurice Merleau-Ponty took it a further step, arguing that cognition is in fact a function of the body – which includes the brain – rather than being located purely in the brain or mind: 'Consciousness is in the first place not a matter of "I think that" but of "I can"' (1962: 137). It is an action in time and space, not just a thought in a Platonic dimension.

These philosophers of phenomenology have been supported more recently by cognitive scientists, many of whom insist that their research shows the extent to which consciousness is as much a matter of the lived body as of the thinking mind. Mark Johnson, for instance, writes that:

> our consciousness and rationality are tied to our bodily orientations and interactions in and with our environment. Our embodiment is essential to who we are,

to what meaning is, and to our ability to draw rational inferences and to be creative. (1987: xxxviii)

It is important to consider this issue of minds versus (or plus) bodies, because in much writing and thinking about what it means to be human, the body tends to be overlooked or translated. First it is turned from itself, a matter of skin, flesh and organs, into a canvas for representation so that the body becomes a signifier of male, female, attractive, homosexual, muscular, disabled, and so on. Next, its physiological and phenomenological qualities are reconfigured as mere signs of cognition. It is one of the lingering effects of Descartes to transform the body into simply the shell in which the thinking *I* lives, or the vehicle in which it travels, and which it reads only in terms of cognition. This is an effect too of what Derrida calls 'logocentrism' – only 'the word' has force, only 'the word' serves to convey us to the world, and the world to us.

BEYOND COGITO

It is quite easy to find counter-examples that demonstrate the extent to which the body is not just a canvas for representation, a dumb sensual appendage to the mind, but is itself a representing subject, carrying the marks of culture. For example, everyone with the physical aptitude to do so learns to walk; but how one walks is determined by many factors – where you live; the period in which you live; and how people of your gender are supposed to walk. Pierre Bourdieu's work on the Kabyle people in Algeria showed that the physical state of individuals was not just a matter of the mechanics of their bodies. Rather, it was a feature of their social identity, an effect of what he calls 'the cultural arbitrary' that shapes the possibilities, even for something as 'natural' and 'normal' as walking. Kabyle men, Bourdieu writes, walk with a 'steady and determined pace', while women are 'expected to walk with a slight stoop' (1977: 94). This is not for any obvious reason except to reinforce the system of values that 'proves' that men are 'manly' and assured, and women are modest and restrained: the purely arbitrary effect of a set of cultural principles and systems of evaluation. These cultural effects come to seem natural through the workings of the **habitus**. Habitus is, in Bourdieu's terms, history turned into nature, i.e., 'denied as such' (Bourdieu 1977: 78). It is, in fact what we can think of as a 'second nature', the individual's mostly unconscious dispositions that emerge from learned behaviours, and structure what the individual is likely to do in any circumstance. Even the movement of the body, as we see above, is an effect of habitus – the thinking, forgetting, conscious and unconscious modes of the person that include body and brain, self and mind.

Some writers, though, have followed Descartes' lead and framed the body as being 'beyond' representation and 'beyond' reason: the locus of feeling, not of consciousness. 'Feeling', as Rauch writes:

> does not have a form; it has to be treated like an inner sensation which can only be understood in terms of the images it triggers. These images do not, however, represent the feeling as such, for they are independently existing representations or fantasies that are merely associated at the moment of pleasure or pain. (1996: para 11)

This is an important issue in understanding the mind/body problem, and the relationship between representation and experience. The body, as Bourdieu noted above, is a cultural site as much as a physical one, and how we express our bodies and their sensations is cultural too. Elaine Scarry, who has researched human pain, points out that in one culture the tendency is to vocalize pain – to cry out – while in other cultures people remain silent under pain (as far as is possible, that is). Which is to say, though it is of the body, it is not pure phenomenon, but is also a matter of culture. Still, she does argue that pain is of a different order from other feelings, like longing or happiness: it has a 'resistance to language':

> physical pain – unlike any other state of consciousness – has no referential content. It is not *of* or *for* anything. It is precisely because it takes no object that it, more than any other phenomenon, resists objectification in language. (1985: 5)

Does this mean that pain cannot be represented, and is not itself a representation of something going on in the body? Richard Rorty suggests that this is the case. He argues that while ideas and attitudes are easily identified as 'mental', pain itself, the neural processes that cause us to feel pain and, say, the muscular contractions that produce the pain, are all considered non-mental. They are the things that will disappear with the disappearance of the body in death, while mental states, reducible as they are to representation, can 'linger on' (Rorty 1980: 17). Language and representation are thus outside the space of pain and, in Wittgenstein's notion, are anyway insufficient for pain. Wittgenstein writes, 'The verbal expression of pain replaces crying and does not describe it' (1958: ss244). It is the kick of the body against the physical assault; but it does not represent the assault or the pain; it is a part of them.

(MIS)PERFORMING THE SELF

I described earlier how our identities are produced as effects of culture and, centrally, of representation. This is true even for our physical bodies: as we saw with the example of the Kabyle people, we 'know' what a man or a woman is because we have representations that tell us what they are, and how they differ (however valid or invalid these 'truths' may be). That knowledge not only informs, it also frames. We 'know' that there are only men and women, and that they are distinct, discrete and different – although as the queer community have made clear, Man and Woman are only the outer points of a continuum of sexual identity, both felt and performed. Those of us who understand ourselves to be only and purely, say, *woman* do this, according to Judith Butler, not because of our body and its shape and parts, but because we *perform* our gender, just as we perform other aspects of our identity. Being, whether we understand it as a mental or a phenomenological state, is the effect of the repetition of a particular representation that, because it is done over and over, actually consolidates our understanding of our own identity. Like rehearsing a play, reiterating gender makes it second nature, makes it 'come naturally', makes it a convincing part of the story of 'me' (Butler 1990: 140) and how I represent myself to myself and others.

Alfred Hitchcock provides examples of this. His movie *Rear Window* (1954) is a narrative as much about the performance (and misperformance) of gender as it is a murder mystery. The male protagonist, Jeff (James Stewart), is trapped in his apartment by a badly broken leg – which, by the way, was caused by his own clumsiness in his work as a photojournalist. He is very 'male' – demanding, aggressive, confident, concerned with the public domain of news and politics – but he is reduced to an 'unmanned' state by his plaster cast that renders him unable to move freely, and is dependent on the services and goodwill of his visiting nurse Stella (Thelma Ritter) and his girlfriend Lisa (Grace Kelly). His attempts to 'be male' by dominating the scene become increasingly petulant and ineffective: he refuses to go to bed, he sulks about his condition, he rejects Lisa's perspective on the world (except where it agrees with his), complains that she is 'frivolous': but he is dependent, vulnerable and rather frivolous himself.

He amuses himself by acting as a voyeur: watching his neighbours and neighbourhood from his eponymous rear window, through binoculars and a powerful zoom lens on his camera. In the process, and with Lisa's help, he realizes he has witnessed a murder. The murderer, Thorwald (Raymond Burr) at first seems to fit the criteria of masculinity. He is powerful and capable, and in control of his situation: able to murder his wife and dispose of her body without arousing suspicion. But he is also represented as vulnerable: when Jeff phones him to threaten him with his knowledge of the crime, Thorwald is frozen, framed within his window and within the camera's (and Jeff's, and the audience's) gaze. This position, the object of the gaze, is the position occupied by women in 1950s movies, but not, typically, by men. His voice and his speech, too, represent his vulnerability. Responding to Jeff he states, helplessly, 'I only have $100 or so,' and then asks, 'What do you want?' – effectively delivering authority to the disembodied male voice at the end of the phoneline.

In the final scenes, Thorwald and Jeff both return to the ·position of masculine dominance – or attempt to. Thorwald discovers who is threatening him, and comes into Jeff's apartment to confront him. But neither is really very effective in this typically male situation. Jeff cannot stop Thorwald from invading his space, and Thorwald cannot at first take advantage of his more active, more powerful body. He stands in the dark and asks, helplessly, 'What do you want from me? What is it you want? Say something' – again handing control of the narrative to Jeff. Finally he moves to attack Jeff who hopelessly, and risibly, tries to hold him back by firing his flashgun at the murderer – something that has more effect than one might expect, but of course cannot actually hold back the darkness. Thorwald reaches him (though a bit blinded by the flash) and wrestles him over the windowsill.

Their incompetent masculine performances do not position them as quintessential 'males', only as rather hopeless characters compulsively rehearsing an idea of masculinity that they cannot sustain. While they act out their roles, Lisa – the glamorous, social butterfly type – has climbed into Thorwald's apartment to retrieve the murdered woman's wedding ring (and thus the proof that she is dead), wrestled with the murderer, and finally saved Jeff. By the very end of the movie, Jeff is asleep in his wheelchair, both legs now in plaster casts; and Lisa is curled comfortably on the bed, pretending to read a book that would please Jeff but actually reading *Harper's Bazaar*. She has broken the rules of feminine identity, but only to a considered extent. She manages to perform as appropriately female – she wears attractive clothes, produces meals, yearns for marriage (this was the 1950s, after all), and avoids pointing out too often to her incompetent boyfriend that she is a successful professional woman capable of straddling the public and the private domain, the active and the passive roles – that she is Derrida's *différance*, embodied.

The point here is that the body is not just a feeling organism; it is a cultural performer. And its performances always fall short of the ideal – in this case, the extreme of either Man or Woman. This is because those ideals are not 'real'; they are the products of ideology, of discourses about what is appropriate to be as a human being, and of representations of those discourses and ideologies.

BODIES VERSUS MINDS

But this does not put to bed the mind/body problem, raised by Descartes, and continuing to exercise philosophers and scientists ever since. It has been reinvigorated in recent years, thanks in no small part to the rise of communication technologies and the questions they raise about the location of the subject.

Earlier I discussed the way in which a photograph both is and isn't 'me'. The main problem it raises is that of location: it generates the 'where am I?' question that we met at the mirror phase. It also raises a problem of time because a 'me' continues to exist in a photograph; whatever else is going on in the subject's life, the image in the photograph just goes on, frozen in time. Paul Virilio writes, 'It's a bit like the baby who, in the photographic print or the Lumière brothers' film, has gone on guzzling his food just as hungrily since the beginning of the twentieth century, even though he long ago died of old age' (2000: 34–5). Still, photos are markers of the truth 'being there', which explains the compulsion to record on film or disk, to put ourselves (literally) in the picture (as performed in the image below). They keep our memories alive, and prove that we too were alive, and were 'there', wherever there might be.

New technologies take this even further. No longer do we blithely agree that being a self means being a soul (thinking or believing) that inhabits a body. Instead, ideas of the self and experiences of being ramify across contexts and concepts: individuals may be cyborgs, inhabitants of MUD universes, 'vactors', transhumans, clones, Six Million Dollar men, or Lara Crofts:

Figure 3.5 © Paul Travers 2006

all those who are not really human, not really machine, and not really cartoon either, but capable of straddling all those formations. The new technologies that make this possible also make it possible for cognition and representation to exist in the machine rather than in the person, raising serious questions about the body/mind problem. While disembodied brains may still be in the realm of science fiction, prosthetic legs that 'think for themselves' are already available, and considerable advances have been made in the development of artificial intelligence. The internet allows people to escape the materiality of their bodies, at least temporarily, and re-emerge as avatars. If this continues so that we really can do without our bodies, we will be able escape its limitations of space and time, aging and disease and, finally, death.

But perhaps our brains and bodies are not so easily separated from one another, either in terms of space and time or in terms of their function. Despite the implications of Descartes' maxim, thinking is not only a matter of the brain or mind. Rather, it is a problem of existence: 'Cognition is a biological phenomenon and can only be understood as such,' write biologists Humberto Maturana and Francisco Varela (1980: 7). We can think, not because we are brains inhabiting dumb bodies, but because we are *em*bodied. Our brains, like our bodies, are material, a necessary property we share with other sentient life forms. Douglas Fox, for example, described recent research that shows the cognitive capacity of a fruit fly. Experiments have shown that flies pay attention to their environment, and their brainwaves, when they are paying attention, 'look uncannily like the ones you see in a human brain when it is paying attention. This is a tantalising discovery. ... What you pay attention to defines how you experience the world from moment to moment' (Fox 2004: 32). Which seems to suggest that fruit flies not only have cognitive capacity, but are also capable of making representations: of defining their worlds.

This is a bit deflating for anyone who clings to the Enlightenment notion that 'man' is the centre of knowledge. If we're not really that different from a humble fruit fly, what is special about us? Not much, it seems: we are just another species of living organism in the world. Certainly we have the capacity to make representations and to interact in both ephemeral and concrete environments, but science suggests this is not unusual. Cognitive functions are the means we use to visualize something that is not present to us: that is, to make a representation of something that remains purely in our mind, as all sentient things do to various degrees. It seems, indeed, that the conditions of representation, the slipperiness of language and the complexities of the human subject are not just the inventions of human culture, but actually apply at the most fundamental biological level. Descartes is correct to identify us as 'things that think' but, according to Maturana and Varela, this is true for all living systems – all are cognitive systems 'and living as a process is a process of cognition' (1980: 13).

This is quite a change from nineteenth century understanding of cognition, expressed by Immanuel Kant in the *Critique of Judgement* as a property of the mind related to reason, and thus divorced from feeling or preference: 'a judgement of taste is not a cognitive judgement and so is not a logical judgement' (1987: 44). Now, though, understandings of cognition have shifted from the idea of it being reason to the idea that it is akin to information processing (Tsur 2002), part of the activity of the brain *and* the body, and how all living organisms respond to their environments. Or, we might say, how they make mental representations.

MENTAL REPRESENTATION

'Mental representation' is the term for how the brain represents and organizes knowledge in a person's memory. It is one of the cognitive functions that make the world real to us, but is not precisely the same as cognition. The latter term refers to the creative shaping of our *con*ceptions of the world, while the former term refers to *per*ception, rather than representation as we have been describing it. The point here is that we are aware of objects only through the ideas that represent them: so that even the most concrete of representations make meaning not because of their own structure or properties, but because someone produced them out of their state of mind, and other people made sense of them in terms of their own states of mind (Crane 2002: 53).

Let's take this a bit further, to explain how cognition, consciousness and mental representation work as physical and cultural activities. We start with the point that the body experiences a *something* – what psychologists call 'sense data' – which is derived from an 'event'. The event may simply be that the body encounters an object, feels (something), and thus has an experience. But the body is aware – or takes notice – of some sense data, and not of others. For instance, if I am engrossed in a movie, I may not notice the mosquito that has landed on my skin. But no matter how engrossed I may be, if I start to have an asthma attack, I become aware that something is going on. I am made conscious of it, and so I take notice and then take action. My body as a living and interacting organism derives information from the sense data, makes a mental representation of what is going on, works cognitively to interact with that event in that environment, generates a conscious awareness, and then derives a cultural outcome. The outcome is how I decide to act on that asthma attack. If I am an anxious person, I may panic and dash for the door and my nebuliser; if I worry about disturbing others, I may creep out of the cinema; if I am fairly relaxed and know that my drugs work, I may just use my inhaler and settle back for the rest of the movie. This is a combination of body, mind and personal tendencies – the habitus – behaving in particular, and contextually specific, ways.

There is considerably more to cognition and consciousness than that, of course, and it has generated a large and complex body of research and writing. Perhaps the most important issue, for the purposes of this book, is that it appears that sense data are not just pieces of information, bits and bytes that produce sensations and experiences. Rather, those sensations and experiences can be understood as being, themselves, representations. They are not simply instances of 'being', but they make meanings because how we represent them to ourselves affects how we actually experience the associated event.

There is, though, a difference between physical and 'purely' representational data. The physical is more obvious: when we look at something outside ourselves, we can see that it is clearly a representation, and not an actuality. If you look at the word 'map', for example, you know you are looking at a representation, not an actuality, because it is only a collection of codes and symbols: squiggles on a page. Those trained to decode them can tell that the squiggles M-A-P together represent the word 'map'. Those not trained see only squiggles; or they may, if imaginative, see a picture in the juxtapositioning of the letters: a highly abstracted hand with lowered thumb, perhaps, or an abstracted axe.

But when it comes to sensory experience, there is no gap between what is represented, and the form – or vehicle – through which it is represented. We cannot examine the individual elements of how an experience presents itself to us; it just *is*. It does not seem to the person experiencing it that it is a representation; that someone else, or you yourself in a different context, might experience it differently.

THE FEELING OF BEING

This raises another question about representation and cognition, one that again comes out of recent scientific investigations. It is the indeterminacy of sensation: and here is where human cognition differs from computer cognition, because it provides considerably more than information. It includes 'the spooky mysterious stuff that no purely informational or functional description of the brain will ever approach' (Gregg 2002). This is **qualia**, a term for mental states that are felt: for example, bodily sensations, or emotions.

Qualia has received considerable attention in recent years (see, for instance, the work of Antonio Damasio 1995, 2000, and Daniel Dennett 1991, 1995), but it builds on much earlier thought about the question of the gap between feeling and thinking. The word is derived from the same root as 'qualitative', and so suggests the subjective and personal rather than the empirical and objective. For some commentators, it is something that cannot be contained by representation. Kant, for instance, suggests that the feeling of being alive exceeds representation; it cannot be reported or recorded in any objective manner (1987: 30). He was writing here about people's responses to aesthetic objects, but his logic is easily transported to the equally subjective domain of the body. Feeling is not about propositional thinking, or the making of a representation; it is not having an idea or wanting something. Rather, it is about how any of these activities feel to the person doing them and so, for Kant, it would not actually be cognition but *Lebensgefühl*, the 'feeling of being alive' (Rauch 1996: para 12).

And yet all those activities are related; Gregg goes on to say that 'By definition, all I ever experience is qualia. Even when I recall the driest, most seemingly qualia-free fact, there is still a palpable what-it-is-like to do so' (2002). For example, you may be plotting a route home to avoid rush hour traffic. This is a cognitive and conscious act: creatively engaging with your world, and fully aware of what you are doing. It relies on your making mental and, quite possibly, material representations – seeing alternative routes in your head, jotting down the name of an alley that will let you cut across town, drawing a mud map of the best way home. It is, in short, an information-processing and an intellectual, conscious activity. But there is a feeling quality to it also: you hold your pencil in a particular way, you feel your body breathing and living in the process, you know that you are engaged in an activity. And the knowing is at once qualia – a feeling-ness that is beyond representation – and a cognitive act, which must be a mental representation.

Take it one step further, and we can suggest that it is possible to identify something particular about human beings, something more than the representational and physiological properties we share with other sentient organisms. This is what it means, and feels, to live in human communities, and how we make choices about the way we engage with others. Richard Rorty describes it thus:

> The problem of consciousness centers around the brain, raw feels, and bodily motions. The problem of reason centers around the topics of knowledge, language, and intelligence – all our 'higher powers'. The problem of personhood centers around attributions of freedom and of moral responsibility. (1980: 35)

Finally, then, this seems to be how we are made. At a cultural level, it is representation and its insistence on difference and deferral that produces us as human subjects. At a physiological level, the mind, itself a product of body and brain, feeling and cognition, produces us as organisms in environments. Interacting, thinking, remembering, feeling, wishing and being, we become subjects; and, up to the point at which we die, we keep becoming subjects, always a little different from who we were just a moment ago.

I will return to the issue of subjectivity in the final chapter, where I discuss the ethical issues at stake in representation and what this means for individuals and groups. In the next chapter, I move attention from the individual to the collective, and discuss how political representation works to make national communities and to make the citizens of those communities.

4 Representation and the political world

So far I have discussed the concept of representation, its function in constituting the world for us, the way representation works in language, and the way representation forms the basis for personal identity. A further, and important, issue is the relationship between representation and politics. How are communities formed, and how does identity circulate within them? How do interest groups access political institutions in order to have some say in their culture? Who is authorized, or entitled to speak in the political institution, and on behalf of whom? How each political community answers such questions will set the terms for the quality of life and its freedom for individual members. For example, whether women are recognized as political subjects, whether people from minority groups have equal access to power, and what sorts of cushions are in place for those who fall out of the system, are all issues that need to be addressed, implicitly or explicitly, by the way in which political representation is organized. This chapter deals with the issue of political representation, and where individuals fit in the domain of government. But before addressing government, I will spend a little time on the notion that every individual must be understood, and must understand themselves to be, part of a larger collective.

COMMUNITIES AND POWER

The collective referred to here is not the taxonomical one of *homo sapiens sapiens* – the community of all human beings – but the smaller and more local one named 'my family', 'my neighbourhood', 'my co-religionists', 'my ethnic group' or 'my nation'. It is the group that is larger than the self, and smaller than the whole. This community provides the individual with a name (I'm a Smith; I'm from the Bronx; I'm Muslim; I'm Latino; I'm French); and that name builds part of the frame around what counts as 'me', cutting me out from the vast horde of *homo sapiens sapiens*, and delimiting the scope of my identity. It also provides me with fellows, those who are like me, and in this way gives me models for how I believe and behave.

This community not only gives me the terms for identity; it also sets restrictions in place around who I can be and what I can do. Restriction is an important issue because community is a state of power, not just an accident of living close to others. It always involves a hierarchy in which individuals are placed; some are dominant and some dominated, some wealthy and some impoverished, some considered 'worthy' and others 'worthless'. It also always involves rules for behaviour, backed up with rewards for behaving appropriately and sanctions for breaking the rules.

The rules that govern any community of any size are, as we saw in Foucault's notion of representation discussed in Chapter 1, backed up by power. For Pierre Bourdieu this is, in the first instance, **symbolic power**. It is part of the representational domain because it makes the absent present, and uses the symbolic properties of language to name, and bring into existence, a community. Bourdieu writes that symbolic power:

> consists in the power to make something exist in the objectified, public, formal state which only previously existed in an implicit state ... The performative power of naming, which almost always comes with a power of representation, brings into existence in an instituted form ... what hitherto existed only as a serial collection of juxtaposed individuals. (1987: 14)

Two senses of the word 'representation' are thus involved in communities. First there is representation as symbolic power, found in the use of language and images to bring something into existence. Second there is representation as delegation, found in the use of a person or organization authorized to stand in for, and speak for, all the members of that community. The extent to which this power shifts from being symbolic to being actual force is determined not by the size of the community, but by the terms under which it exists.

For instance, the 'serial collection of juxtaposed individuals' that, in Western cultures, is called 'the nuclear family' is governed implicitly and internally by relations that can often only be understood as force: the power a parent has to control the children, the power a violent adult has over his or her partner and children. Another power over the family comes from the state; this may be both external and explicit power that is encoded in laws and also articulated in the norms, or values, supported by the state. These laws and norms set out what constitutes a family and what are appropriate relations within that family. A family marked by violence will – when identified – be treated first with symbolic power. A social worker may spend time explaining to members how to engage with each other, for example. If that doesn't work, force is likely to be applied: the children forcibly removed from the home, or the abusive partner arrested. Communities, then, are managed by representational, or symbolic, power – the power to say that a particular group constitutes a community, and to determine what sort of community it is. They are also governed by other sorts of power – that of the law, that of social norms and mores, that of brute force, and that of the small local tussles in everyday life about who 'we' are, and how 'we' should be represented and represent ourselves.

MAKING THE COMMUNITY

Individual people become members of a community in one of two ways: by being necessarily part of it (by birth, for instance), or by choosing to belong. A person may be born as a subject of, say, Britain – membership without choice – but choose to identify with a particular football team; or with the community of artists; or with the Closed Brethren Christian community. It is important though to remember that membership of a community isn't really based on an either (inevitable) or (self-selected) basis. The extent to which we really choose our communities is very limited. Our choices are always more limited than they appear to us to have been. If closely examined, it will be possible to see a certain inevitability in our life choices and our identity. For instance, I choose a particular football team thinking that it is purely a matter of free choice; but an analyst investigating my life might be able to point out that I really chose it because I live near that team's headquarters, or because my mother was a great fan of that team, or because my mother was a great fan of that team's main rivals and I chose them to annoy her. Or it might be that the newspaper I commonly read or the television station I commonly watch favours that team, and so they have come to feel like my home team. Maybe I have always had a soft spot for the underdog and this team always loses, valiantly; or I have always identified with winners, and this team is always in the top of the league. There could be many other factors, equally traceable back to non-random reasons for my preference. On the surface they may seem entirely random, but in fact are all tightly connected to my life history, and the many factors that have made me who I am.

So when it comes to the constitution of a collective, one of the terms for membership might be choice, however inevitable that choice may in fact be: this is particularly the case for social collectives – religious, leisure and professional groups. But in most collectives we are pretty much automatically members, like it or not: especially the accident-of-birth ones. You *just happened* to be born into a particular family, in a particular nation, and that means you are a member of that family and that nation. Of course you can change this in later life – marry out of your family and cut all ties with them; emigrate and become a citizen of another nation. However, you will always bear the traces of your origin. Your genetic make-up is tied to your birth parents, even if you have never met them or haven't spoken to them for years. And your place of birth will always be on official documents, even if you manage to change your accent and otherwise blend in perfectly with your new national community.

An area where there is no choice is membership of a political community. You may have decided to drop out of life entirely – hold no bank accounts, have no employment, no driver's licence, no home, no friends. But even if you do manage to avoid all other connections, you have to be governed from some point, and some body larger than yourself must be in a position to take responsibility for you. This need not be benign, of course: the responsibility they take might simply be to imprison you. Nor need it be active: it might be that the only actual care you ever receive from your government in a long and neglected life is after your death, when they find, scoop up and bury your body. But to be a human being – or rather, to be recognized as such – you must belong to a recognized collective: because the alternative is too awful. As Hannah Arendt wrote, 'a man who is nothing but a man has lost the very qualities which make it possible for other people to treat him as a man' (1966: 300).

ON NOT BEING VISIBLE

How can a person lose the qualities that make it possible for others to treat him as a man? One way is to do as I suggested above: drop out entirely. By doing so, you reduce yourself to what Giorgio Agamben (1998), following Aristotle, calls **bare life**. Bare life, or simple being, is what we have in common with all living beings. Aristotle's term for it is *zoë*: life outside of politics and other social interaction, the simple inner and physical being of 'me-ness'. It is officially silent: only political life has access to speech, but bare life is, like animals, mute.

A second way to lose those qualities is not to be seen at all by the authorities because you are not represented by them, and can make no representations to them. There are many examples of the practical invisibility of those not politically represented, or not identified with a formal governmental system. One comes out of the invasion/settlement of Australia: although the various indigenous peoples had lived there for millennia, and had settlements all over the continent, the British authorities who arrived in the late eighteenth century did not acknowledge them in any formal way. In fact, they named Australia a *terra nullius*, an empty land, a land without people. Of course there were people there: they saw them, had dealings with them, and sometimes massacred them. The point is not that the indigenous people were not *actually* visible and present, but they were not *practically* visible and present because, as far as the British authorities were concerned, they had no system of government and no authorized identity, hence no official presence.

It was not only in Australia that this happened, of course. Comedian Eddie Izzard, in his 1998 show *Dress to Kill*, discusses how the British Empire established itself: 'We stole countries with the cunning use of flags. Just sail around the world and stick a flag in.' He then acts out the scene, taking the side first of the British spokesperson, and then the spokesperson for the invaded country:

'I claim India for Britain!'
'You can't claim us; we live here. Five hundred million of us.'
'Do you have a flag?'
'We don't need a bloody flag. This is our country.'
'No flag, no country. You can't have one. That's the rule that I've just made up. And I'm backing it up with this gun.'

The rule of government is the rule of nomination (manifested through a flag or other sign of government) and the rule of power (the bigger gun will always rule). This is precisely how Australia could become 'Australia' rather than an island continent made up of dozens of territories, as it was prior to the British arrival. There was no 'flag' (metaphorically or actually), there was no government that the British recognized as such, despite some 50,000 years of organized community life with laws and customs, traditions and symbolic life, and no representative body that could speak for the local inhabitants. *No flag, no country*. Similarly, *no representative government, no people*.

THE POWER OF FLAGS

A flag is both an actual and a metaphorical sign designed to collect within that sign a mass of disparate people, and to produce in them a sense of us-ness (and, by extension, a sense that others are outsiders). They do this by a sort of sleight of hand, convincing people of their profound importance, and blinding them to the fact that they are just bits of fabric, usually designed by committee, and stitched together by ordinary people in factories. The flags in Figure 4.1, for example, are sold cheaply from a pavement stall (see over), ostensibly to celebrate the national football team, though of course they do multiple duty as representation of the nation, of the team, and of the group of fans. Despite the very banal nature that flags really have, the power of analogy to draw connections

Figure 4.1 Flags on display during the FIFA World Cup, London (2006)

between the flag and the nation, and the power of metonymy that allows the flag to stand in for the whole notion, means they are treated with reverence.

Or with disdain, of course. During the Vietnam War, for example, Americans protesting against the war often burnt the US flag to signify their distaste for the effects of patriotism and nationalism that had led to the invasion of a much smaller sovereign nation. Then, following the 2001 attacks on New York and Washington and the subsequent invasion of Afghanistan and then Iraq, the nation seemed overnight to blossom with national flags, flying from every car, shop entrance and front yard: a statement of aggressive patriotism as well as support for the US troops who had been sent into war. At the same time, of course, in Iraq and Palestine – and no doubt in other protesting nations – angry people burnt the US flag in what seems to be a metonymic understanding of its representative power. That is, by burning the tiny part (the flag) they symbolically burnt the whole (the nation). An actually insignificant object, through the symbolic power of representation, is able to 'make something exist in the objectified, public, formal state' (Bourdieu 1987: 14) and make it visible as an entity that exists not only for its members, but also for others. Unlike the indigenous Australians who had no flag (no symbols of national community that could be recognized by the British), the US, whether as 'us' or as 'them', exist visibly in the presence of their flag.

MAKING THE NATION

The principle of power that produces communities out of collections of discrete individuals has been of enormous interest to philosophers and other theorists over many centuries. Plato's *The Republic* is an attempt to make sense of how to manage the organized collective that is community. So too is the Pentateuch, the first five books of the Bible, where the rules for what may be done and by whom, and who may speak and for whom, are set out in considerable detail. The Code of Hammurabi, which dates from around 1780 BCE, is another of the several very ancient documents that combine law, philosophy and political theory, and that demonstrate the very long history of concern for what makes a community, and how it can be sustained. At the heart of the history of political community is the struggle between, on the one hand, the attempt to behave as though 'we' have 'always existed' – to locate the origins of the community in the dim or even mythological past – and on the other to acknowledge the need to construct the community by active representations.

The interesting aspect of this, from the point of view of someone concerned with representation, is the very close connection between the structure of the political community and the structure of language. Both are media of representation, or modes and forms in which representation operates. Ernesto Laclau shows this explicitly, using the discourse of language to make sense of the constitution of communities. He points out that just as linguistic signs exist only in a relational context, so too social identity only exists – only has meaning – in what he calls 'a set of discursive relations' (1988: 254). We have seen in earlier chapters that, although of course there is reality outside language, we can only access that reality when it is mediated by and articulated through representation. So too, Laclau suggests, although of course we have identity in the sense of bare life – we are alive and breathing – our identity can't be grasped, asserted or recognized outside the context of a formally constituted community.

THE MASTER SIGNIFIER

Laclau and Mouffe suggest that the way to understand this is to see the idea of nation as being what they term a 'master signifier' (Laclau and Mouffe 1985: 127). The master signifier is the term that governs the possibility of meaning in a particular discourse, and provides meaning to all the other terms associated with it. The chain of associations in binary logic that we saw in Chapter 2 works much this way, with God being the master signifier that anchors the whole chain, and gives every element within it not only meaning, but differential value.

The master signifier of nation simplifies society because it collapses the many objective (or actual) differences into a sameness, in the form of the shared identity provided by that master signifier. For example, I live in a town of some 300,000 people, each of them with a discrete personal history and personal identity. We are all divided from one another by being different ages and generations, different genders and sexualities; by speaking different languages; by coming from different nations and different ethnic groups (almost half of the population were either born overseas themselves, or are children of immigrants); by having different levels of income, different education, different jobs and professions and so on. Although it is a comparatively little community, it is marked by many objective differences. But the master signifier that is the name 'Canberra', and is objectified in the local government that shares its name, provides a way of unifying us into an idea of sameness: we possess the shared identity of being 'Canberran'.

Of course there are 'real' or objective similarities among us; those eligible to do so vote for the same candidates to become our political representatives; we worry about the surface of the same potholed road; we experience the same weather patterns; when bushfires are around we all inhale the same smoke and worry about the same threat. These are some of the 'real' shared elements; and they are, arguably, no more important in the constitution of the community than the purely 'representational' shared elements – those that emerge from our all being connected to the master signifier that is named Canberra. We have far more differences than similarities, but the master signifier produces the effect of a unified subject position and a common political identity in which 'we all' have shared interests and a shared investment.

This concept can be seen, in concrete terms, in the way particular institutions that exist apparently to serve the national interest are just as much involved in making, as in supporting, the national identity. I pointed out above that Australia did not exist prior to its being named as part of the process of colonization. The island continent has been around for eons, and has been inhabited, according to the anthropological and paleontological data, for something like 50,000 years. But it did not exist as a representative nation until 1901, when at the point of Federation it was named 'Australia'.

In much the same manner, it still does not exist except in the discourses about it, the practices that say it is a nation (such as trade, diplomatic and security relationships), and the institutions that 'prove' its existence. We know that Australia exists because there are institutions that bear its name: the *Australian* Broadcasting Commission, *Australian* Film Commission or *Australia* Council for the Arts. Its flag distinguishes it from all other countries, as do its rituals and its stories of itself. To use Laclau and Mouffe's term, these relationships, discourses, practices and institutions are what put content into the empty master signifier 'Australia'.

The point is that there is no 'real' Australia, any more than there is a 'real' France or a 'real' Iraq. Each nation is the product of a whole range of signifying and representative practices, and of a history of the organization of people and power. They exist only in description and in practice; a different description, a different practice, and they cease to exist in that form and become something else. We have seen examples of this recently in the Soviet Union, Yugoslavia and Czechoslovakia, all of which in the past decades have ceased to be 'themselves' and become 'something else'. In the rush to convince populations that their nation is a necessary and autonomous collective of people with a shared history, traditions and interests, national commentators tend to overlook the youth of the idea of nation. Up to the Enlightenment, nations did not exist as we now understand them; rather there were collectives held together by religious organizations, by loyalty to a sovereign, or even by feudal ties. Any nation-state that now exists is only, in that state, a couple of hundred years old, so the narratives used to prove the antiquity of the nation, and hence its claims to land and loyalty, are a bit specious.

Just as there is a tendency to overlook the recency of any nation, so too the considerable (if not necessarily conscious) effort that goes into proving that a community is necessarily 'a people' tends to be unremarked. But a nation has to be *made* evident because 'the nation' is an empty concept – empty of necessity or actuality, though not empty of use value. This effort can be seen in the multiple images any nation has for itself: its flags and crests, its advertising programs, its cultural production. One such example can be seen in this image of a McDonalds sign in Suva, Fiji (over page). It doesn't only represent (stand in for) the McDonalds corporation, and doesn't only represent (make present through signification) the possibility of buying fast food, but also represents (reiterates) a distinctively Fijian concept: the cheerful greeting 'Bula' that doubles as a marker of nation and a tourist sign. Similarly, in the centre of Wellington, New Zealand, the roadside bollards have been crafted to resemble the *koru*, a new fern frond, that is also a symbol of the nation. These bollards have multiple duties: they are aesthetic compared with the up-and-down concrete block that is the usual bollard; they make the statement – for those who know the code – that 'this is New Zealand'; they protect the pavement from passing traffic, of course; and they draw attention to a particular national difference.

Both these images provide instances of a public object that is both practical and representational. They serve a social function; but more than that, they serve a national function, setting aside a particular sign to stand in for the nation, and in that process to shore up the nation's identity. Laclau insists that 'any representation ... is an attempt to constitute society, not to state what it is' (1990: 82). In public institutions, objects, discourses and

Figure 4.2 A McDonalds sign in Suva, Fiji

Figure 4.3 Roadside bollards in Wellington, New Zealand

practices, we can see attempts not to *describe* the nations, but to *make* them visible and real.

TOWARDS REPRESENTATIVE GOVERNMENT

The most powerful community to which any of us belong is the national government, and in the West the idea of government has what is virtually an automatic connection with representative democracy. Indeed, 'The idea of representation is central to parliamentary democracy', Marion Sawer and Gianni Zappalà write in the introduction to their edited book, because 'Without the belief that others can somehow represent them, citizens will withdraw their trust from parliamentary institutions' (2001: 1).

It is, though, a modern phenomenon. There have of course always been ways of governing groups. Perhaps in pre-history the very tiny size of social groups made it possible to manage on the basis of negotiation (though observations of primate communities suggest force as a more likely basis for community). God was invoked early in recorded history as both the ultimate force and the ultimate guarantor of a ruling authority's power. And running alongside the theocratic notion was a constant tussle between the various powerful entities (royal families, senior politicians, members of the nobility, the priesthood) and the people who, although almost always officially powerless, still had the capacity to revolt against the government, and so always at least had to be taken into account, if not consulted. None of these is a representative system of government. The earliest gesture towards democracy is found in ancient Greece: if we can give that name to the way the elite of Athens managed their society. In fact theirs was closer to participation than representative democracy since all members eligible to vote (and they were few) in fact *participated* directly in government, rather than leaving the decisions up to their spokesperson.

Representative government as we now know it first emerged, though in a very protean form, during the Medieval period in Europe. Although monarchs then held considerable power, they could not govern without the agreement (and the armies) of the nobles; and they were bound too by the authority of the Church. Because of this, the beginnings of political representation can be seen in the process of 'the monarch summoning the great men of the realm to give their assent to certain taxes he wished to levy' (Schwartz 1988: 2). Of course very few people were involved in the representation – only the wealthy and powerful – but even this limited form was put on hold at the end of the feudal period.

The next historical period was marked by the shift to what some historians call the age of absolutism, when kings, nobles and the Church battled it out for sovereignty. But there were few real checks on the power of the monarch now. Though the Church was still powerful, it no longer had the sort of influence it had wielded during the medieval period; and as the duchies and principalities began to consolidate, the nobles had to cede some of their authority to the sovereign. Many European parliaments were dismissed or disempowered: the French Estates-General, for instance, were not called from 1614 to 1789 (Birch 1971: 30), and the seventeenth-century French king Louis IV identified himself so fully with the nation France that he famously claimed to *be* that nation: '*l'état, c'est moi*' ['I am the state'].

The turbulence of this period led to social protest and revolution, and to socio-political changes that undermined the power of the monarch, and shifted some of the power to the people. The issue that arose and needed to be resolved was how to connect the *person* (each discrete and particular individual) with the rather more abstract notion of the *citizen*: how to make persons present in the life of government, and how to re-conceptualize the relationship between people and rulers. The gradual move to a more democratic system meant the people finally had some say in the government. But how to manage that say?

THE NEW DEMOCRACY

Even democratic systems set limits on power. Under representative government the power of the people is limited by the need to trust their delegate and to leave the matter of government up to her or him. The power of the monarch was limited by his or her need to achieve the consent of the people. Indeed, even now the power of delegates is limited by the three-to-five year term any democratic government hold. Any longer, Ankersmit suggests, and representatives might be tempted to go against the electorate's wishes (2003: 338, n5). Despite the limits, representation still seemed a good option. For the people it could appear as at least a toe in the door of government; and monarchs too could see it as a better option than competing with other extremely powerful counter-authorities, like the Church or the nobles. Indeed, Nancy Schwarz wrote, 'Modern political representation starts as a device of political rule from the center, in the territorial ruler's search for human sovereignty' (1988: 2).

With the move towards representative government came philosophical speculation on what constitutes good government. The first important issue was, does the representative stand in for the people, or for the throne? Thomas Paine, Thomas Hobbes, John Locke, John Stuart Mill, Jean-Jacques Rousseau and others insisted that government must represent the people. Locke (1975 [1690]) spoke for majority rule on the basis that the people voting would be essentially reasonable. His argument was that people first agree to come together and form a society, and then they agree on and form a government. If this government-by-consent loses the consent of the people by not making appropriate decisions, then the people have an implicit right to discard that government. Stuart Mill (1869) also advocated representative democracy. Unusually for the time, and perhaps for now, he was very concerned that minority opinions should get a hearing, and be represented alongside more widespread views (Mill 1975: 256). Paine wrote in his 1792 treatise *Rights of Man* that combining representation with democracy results in the fairest and most inclusive system of government; and 'the easiest form of government, to be understood' (1969: 232–3) – and he put his energies into helping to draft the American Declaration of Independence, as evidence of the practical possibilities of democracy.

THE PROBLEM OF DEMOCRACY

Thomas Hobbes responded to the question of representative government with a major treatise, *Leviathan* (1651), that wrestles with the issue of power. He pointed out that:

> A multitude of men are made *one* person when they are by one man, or one person, represented; so that it be done with the consent of every one of that multitude in particular. For it is the *unity* of the representer, not the *unity* of the represented, that maketh the person *one*. (1947: 127)

This suggests two answers to the question, in which direction power should flow? The first is that because each person is effectively forced into the social system and brought under the authority of **Leviathan** (Hobbes' metaphor for the commonwealth, or state), power flows from the government to the people ('the unity of the representer' taking precedence). The second answer, on the other hand, suggests that Leviathan is not simply in the place of a sovereign or other authorized ruler; rather, Leviathan is bound by the will of the people (representing only 'with the consent of every one of that multitude'). Unfortunately, the former tends to carry more weight in most analyses of Hobbes' view of representative democracy. This is because he insists that, in the interests of security and a more effective life, people relinquish their individual autonomy to a social authority that will organize things on their behalf. This is the famous (or notorious) '**social contract**' by means of which civil society and representative government are born, and the people are liberated from the yoke of the old system of sovereign government. Along with representative government, though, comes obligation – the obligation to be ruled by Leviathan who is, as we saw above, at the same time the people's representative and the people's dictator.

I noted above that each individual subject, in order to be a subject (a recognized human being), must be a member of a civil society. The concept of the social contract suggests that each of us willingly contracts in to the community. The problem is, it is not really a contract because we have no opportunity to negotiate the terms of the contract, and because there is no sunset clause and no way out: once you have contracted in to the civil society, you are bound by your 'contract' (Pateman 1985: 42). Nor is it a fair contract (if any non-negotiated contract could be said to be fair): women and members of minority groups, as a great deal of research has shown, enter the social contract as second class or second rate members. They are barely allowed in, and then only on terms that do not benefit them – but if they don't enter then they have no formal existence. This is hardly an acceptable notion of representative government, though it still, in many ways, constitutes the basis of civil society and how we all live in communities.

The problems of a Hobbesian democracy were not unremarked by Rousseau, who was entirely opposed to representative government, and insisted that participatory government was the only appropriate approach. This is a system of government where everyone eligible to vote participates personally and actively in all decisions. Rousseau insisted in *The Social Contract* (1762) that proper representation exists only when the people are fully embodied in government: in other words, when they and not their representatives are making the decisions. Indeed, he saw political representation as illegitimate on the grounds that it excluded citizens from the political community (Rousseau 1968: II.1, III.15).

However, though participation and full presence in all aspects of social life might be an attractive ideal, it is hardly a useful premise for a workable system of government. The Peter Cook movie, *The Rise and Rise of Michael Rimmer* (1970), uses this as a plot and shows how impossible, and how ludicrous, participatory government can be. The eponymous Rimmer rises from nowhere to become first an important member of government, and then the prime minister. His platform is full participation and, to ensure that everyone genuinely has a say about Britain's government, every possible issue goes to a referendum. Finally, of course, the people become fed up with constantly having to make decisions about the minutiae of government, and they insist on passing authority back – not just to the government but to Rimmer himself. By the end of the movie he has become a dictator, by the 'will of the people'.

BACK TO REPRESENTATION

Not surprisingly, perhaps, representative democracy has been more widely instituted than has participatory government. But while it brings the people into the process of government, it does so only in a very limited way. The representatives are the only ones physically present in government, and only ones making decisions – which are not necessarily the decisions that the majority of the constituents would have chosen. Moreover, the representative does not necessarily represent his or her constituents in any useful way. After all, only one human being is elected to stand in for a whole group, a mixture of men and women, young and old, homosexual and heterosexual, and of varying language and ethnic origins.

This problem has also received considerable attention from theorists. Some argue that if that one person fitted a median view of the collective – meeting the average of all those many differences – then she or he would be better equipped to stand in for the whole. This is the **mirror notion** of representation: the idea that parliament should be a mirror of the population as a whole, with different groups and interests represented on a proportional basis. But the individual who fitted the norm would still be unlikely to represent all interests equally. Suppose there is a woman member of parliament who is Asian and gay and a trained welder – for what community of interest is she an effective substitute? How can she speak for – make present – all those groups of whom she can be considered a member, let alone everyone else in her constituency – say, Caucasian professional men heterosexual in preference.

Even if we could achieve a very good fit between the individual representatives and the population as a whole – say, in a very homogeneous electoral district – there is still an issue of how well the representative would represent the members. A parliamentarian may be an embodied likeness, because on demographic measures they fit the bill, but they will they not necessarily speak for those they apparently represent. Suppose my putative politician above was for some reason vehemently against Asian immigration, or opposed to trade union actions: in that case she would be an embodied likeness for those groups, but would lack self-conscious likeness because she does not represent the interests of her groups. One example of the difference between embodied and self-conscious likeness is found in the UK prime minister from 1979 to 1990, Margaret Thatcher; she was certainly a woman and thus embodied the representation of women, but cannot be said to have governed with women's interests in mind.

As well as such obvious limits on the capacity of delegates to represent their constituents, there are other problems with the practicalities of representative government. For one thing, voters have only one vote, once every three to five years. In many nations, that vote can only be cast for one of several people who have already been pre-selected by the political parties. This means the candidates represent the party to the people, and are responsible to both party and people, resulting in split loyalties and split identities. Claude Lefort, reflecting on this system, argues that the move away from the sovereign has not really resulted in democratic power but an 'empty space' (1988), because neither the people, nor the parties, nor the lobby groups, nor the bureaucrats, nor the caucus clearly have the capacity to govern in a representative fashion.

Still, an empty space is one that can be inhabited. Representation gives authority to political delegates to transport the old discourse of sovereignty – the virtually untrammelled power of the sovereign – to that empty space. This can be done when governments come up with and articulate a conception of law that is based on the idea of the will of the people, however deferred and diffused their will or power may in fact be, rather than being based on the preservation of central power.

Perhaps the biggest drawback to representative democracy is the fact that the principle of representation on the one hand brings the ordinary person, 'me', into the sphere of government, and on the other hand excludes that individual. *I* am present in government, but only at a remove, in the person of my representative, and I have no voice; I can only accept the decisions ostensibly made in my name. Evidence suggests that the public recognize the limits of the system: the competing imperatives faced by representatives, the divided loyalties, the lack of a fit between representative and represented, and so on. As Slavoj Zizek puts it, democracy is marked by 'a certain fetishistic split: *I know very well* (that the democratic form is just a form spoiled by stains of 'pathological' imbalance), *but just the same* (I act as if democracy were possible)' (1991: 168).

Because after all, what are the alternatives to representative democracy? So we continue to cast our votes for candidates we may or may not trust, who may or may not resemble us or hold an adequate representative likeness, or speak for our interests; because the alternatives are the exhausting forms of anarchy or participatory democracy, or the possibly brutal regimes of the sovereign or the central state. We may not like or trust them, but we accept it as the worst system, except for all the others (to paraphrase Churchill's famous dictum).

THE PROBLEM OF PRESENCE

Many of these concerns about representative democracy can be read through Jacques Derrida's writings on representation and presence. The problem for individuals in representative democracy is the same problem that emerges in any representative site: the disconnect between the actual and the abstract, the concrete and the represented. Derrida points out that representation, whether in language or in politics, promises to deliver presence – to re-present, or bring back into presence something that was there. There is buried in this concept what in *Of Grammatology* (1974) he calls 'the metaphysics of presence' – the belief that behind the surface of representation is the 'truth' of the real world. Representative government promises us that behind the evidence of my exclusion from authority is the actual presence of me, the citizen, in the workings of government. Of course it cannot deliver that; but the difference between the promise of metaphysics and the experience of the empty space of representative democracy leaves me hungry for participation, and annoyed by my government.

What Derrida's metaphysics of presence reminds us is that politics is not really concerned with the ordinary everyday me that is the actual presence. Rather it is interested in the *idea* of me, the political body: backed up as this idea is by the metaphysical notion of a rational, sensible, participatory citizen (not the noisy, needy, physical being of bare life). The political domain is not well-suited to take care of or satisfy the needs of our actual – our non-political – life because it is interested only in the political self; we however, in our day-to-day experience, are interested in our basic – our bare – life. We forget that there is, for representation, no actual presence behind the form. Though as human beings we possess both political and bare life, they do not occupy the same social position; they are not, for representative government, the same thing or requiring of the same attention.

On the threshold between my lived, embodied, inner self and my represented, abstract, outer self, my identity is both formed and deformed. It is here that I am found and lost. It is here that my expectations of political representation are both raised and dashed. But it is also here that demands can be made, as citizens, for the needs of bare life. We can speak, in our citizen identity, for our own and others' 'bare' needs.

SPEAKING FOR OTHERS

What is involved when someone speaks for, or otherwise stands in for, others? This happens constantly in contemporary society: agents speak for their clients; solicitors and barristers represent their clients; politicians represent their electorates; and civil servants or peak body members represent their departments, or their interest groups. What is at stake in each case is firstly the significatory process involved in standing in for others (i.e., the meanings that are made by the choice of representatives); and next the participatory processes (i.e., how the representative actually acts for those for whom she or he is standing). The representative is always speaking for someone else: and if you are spoken for, you are yourself not speaking, and hence not heard. In the case of delegated representation – that category that includes literary agents, lawyers or sales representatives – the agent acts in the place of, and in the interests of, their principal. In most cases the agent is required to follow the interests of their principal (though, as A.H. Birch points out, legal representatives are also bound by the ethical codes of the legal association, by law and by the requirements of the courts). But symbolic representatives – those elected to represent our interests in parliament – are not bound by the wishes of their principals/constituents (Birch 1971: 16).

Here is a problem at the heart of political representation: those represented are silenced and very possibly ignored at the very point at which they are (apparently) brought into the place of power (Thomassen 2006). Bourdieu wrote about the impossibility of being heard, as an ordinary citizen:

> If I, Pierre Bourdieu, a single and isolated individual, speak only for myself, say 'you must do this or that, overthrow the government or refuse Pershing missiles', who will follow me? But if I am placed in statutory conditions such that I may appear as speaking 'in the name of the masses' ... that changes everything. (1991: 212)

Gilles Deleuze takes up the same complaint in a transcribed conversation between himself and Michel Foucault, where he argues about the radical limits of representation (in Foucault 1972). One problem Deleuze notes is that it is practically impossible to achieve reforms under representative government: if representatives make an attempt to reform the systems on behalf of others, all that is likely to result is a new division of power, but no real beneficial changes. He is being a touch disingenuous here, perhaps – there are many instances we can suggest where practical reforms have been achieved in areas like the position of minority groups, quality of service provision and the treatment of women. However, it is difficult to find any examples of sustained reform leading to greater access to government on the part of the people, or a genuine redistribution of power.

In fact, those representing us in parliament can claim to be entitled to ignore even our expressed will on the grounds that they 'know better'. Edmund Burke, in 1774, presented his Address to the Electors of Bristol in which he argued that 'members of parliament owe the electorate their informed judgement rather than the slavish following of local prejudice or majority opinion' (Sawer and Zappalà 2001: 4): a view still evident in the arrogance with which parliamentary representatives have been known to treat those for whom they are the delegates. A recent example of 'knowing better' and ignoring the will of the people they were elected to represent was seen in the USA, the UK and Australia in the early part of this century, when the governments invaded Iraq despite huge public protests. Their refusal to listen to the people was based on their 'better knowledge' – especially knowledge of Iraq's weapons of mass destruction – weapons that subsequently proved not to exist at all, but too late to prevent the invasion.

The idea that political representatives are bound, either wholly or partly, to the interests of their principals (we, the people) is not borne out by recent history. Individual representatives really have no obligation to follow the wishes of those they were elected to represent. In fact, they have the capacity to make rules that are binding on those same people, whether those rules are in their interests or not. We can think of the complaints often levied against (especially) conservative governments that, though elected by, and in the interests of 'the people', in fact they govern in the interests of big business. Even when corruption is not an issue, it is very difficult for any representative to represent the interests of their constituents. For one thing, there is never just *an* interest, clear, held by all, and non-contradictory. In the USA, the UK and Australia, for instance, the same constituents who were strongly opposed to the war in Iraq were also strongly opposed to terrorism, and the governments were able to claim that they were fulfilling the need for security, while denying the demand for peace. There is never an obvious path to follow, only *paths* marked by interest, probable risk or likely profit; paths laid out by pressure groups and lobbyists, the personal conviction of the representative, the insistence of the party, and many other issues.

One of those issues is the capacity of groups and individuals to capture the attention of their delegate. This shows yet another limit on the actual representative-ness of representative democracy: those most in need of sound representation in the seats of power are typically those ignored. Bourdieu writes that since political participation depends on the ownership of leisure time and cultural capital (1991: 172–3), the more economic, social and cultural capital a group possesses, the greater is their ability to participate in politics, and to ensure that their interests receive political attention. And, of course, the less a group's members have these abilities, the more likely it is that they will rely on 'professional' representatives who are as likely not to attend to their interests as to take them seriously. Government is, effectively, a no-win option for the people, and therefore:

Modern democratic society seems to me, in fact, like a society in which power, law and knowledge are exposed to a radical indetermination, a society that has become the theatre of an uncontrollable adventure. (Lefort 1986: 305)

We will trace this uncontrollable adventure in the next chapter, in a discussion of the role of the media and art in representation.

5 Representation in the consciousness industries: art and the mass media

L et me start with Friedrich Nietzsche:

> the contrast between this real truth of nature and the lie of culture that poses as if it were the only reality is similar to that between the eternal core of things, the thing-in-itself, and the whole world of appearances. (1967: 61)

This chapter explores the 'lie of culture' and its relationship with the inaccessible and limitless 'real truth of nature'. The space in society perhaps most committed to 'the whole world of appearances' is what Stuart Cunningham and Graeme Turner have called 'the **cultural industries**' or 'the **consciousness industries**'. This is the home of art and mass media, the industry sector that produces and disseminates commodities that sell 'ways of thinking, ways of seeing, ways of talking about the world' (Cunningham and Turner 1997: 6).

SIBLING RIVALRY

Of course the act of collapsing art and the media into one sector is itself a representation, using a term to signify and thus set aside two really quite different sites of endeavour. The fields do have many features in common: both hope to woo, please, surprise, captivate and otherwise engage their audiences. Both self-consciously use the things of the world or the imagination – or both – to produce a statement, be it in the form of a news paper article, a painting, a poem, a TV advertisement, a song or a movie. But their differences are marked too, so much so that they are more like sibling rivals than like differing aspects of one identity. In the eyes of the mass media, art can seem the domain of the dilettante – where a great deal of self-indulgent expression goes on and resources are wasted, compared with, say, the news media that serves a serious purpose. The media claims to present a 'balanced view' (Hall 1977: 342) unlike art that (and here they are channelling Kant) does not rely on reason, does not act responsibly within society (channelling Plato), and is inefficient (channelling Schoenburg). The media present their work as a window on the world, capable of showing things as they really are. Art is happy to 'get it wrong' by breaking the rules or rupturing conventions, but the mass media is concerned with 'getting it right'. Artists will follow their instincts or an aesthetic whim; media practitioners will check facts, structure products to connect with audiences, or follow an expected story arc. And where art tends to shrug off social obligation in the interests of being able to pursue ideas in an autonomous manner, the mass media is entirely invested in society. Indeed, television in particular is held up as a significant social site, the contemporary version of the agora, or the meeting place in which the big issues of the day can be debated. As Stuart Cunningham writes, 'Television is the "glue" that holds together much of our sense of ourselves as a society; it is the main platform on which whatever passes as public debate and collective sense-making takes place' (1997: 90).

Art counters the criticisms offered by the mass media, and returns them with interest. For art, the mass media has sold out to Mammon, lacks creative integrity, fails to explore the potential of the available form, and turns audiences into what Theodor Adorno called 'cultural dupes' – passive consumers of whatever representations the media might choose to make. Rather than being genuinely 'objective', it simply offers a dominant perspective, presenting the mainstream views as the true, neutral and therefore the generally 'acceptable' ones (Bourdieu 1975: 38). In short, many theorists saw the mass media as guilty of 'habituating [the masses] to an unproductive, powerless existence livened only by consuming the latest product from the cultural industries' (Turner 1997: 294). Art, on the other hand, its supporters claim:

> permits us to see fiction as fiction, to see the fictiveness or contingency of the world. It reveals the idea of order which we imaginatively impose on reality. Plainly stated, the world is what you make of it. The fact of the world is a *factum*: a deed, an act, an artifice. (Critchley 2005: 58)

However, the differences between them are being eroded by changes in practice, by the effects of the economic field, and by the blurring of distinctions that has been actuated by the forces of convergence, and what we still call the 'new' technologies. A sculptor may now be a media practitioner, making and distributing ephemeral images of 'objects' in space; a news company may provide support for short films and animations; advertisers may use the news of the day to frame the selling of their products; and video game producers may incorporate both poetry and contemporary social comment. So the old divisions cannot be as easily sustained as they were, as the semiotician and novelist Umberto Eco writes:

> Once upon a time there were the mass media, and they were wicked, of course, and there was a guilty party. Then there were the virtuous voices that accused the criminals. And Art (ah, what luck!) offered alternatives, for those who were not prisoners of the mass media. Well, it's all over. We have to start from the beginning, asking one another what's going on. (1986b: 150)

That is to say, the space between art and the mass media is closing up.

FAMILY RESEMBLANCES

This is not to suggest that they are the same, of course, in any absolute sense, or that the criticisms each field has traditionally made of the other have disappeared. They are, to use Wittgenstein's term, connected more by family resemblance than actual identity, and their values, discourses and practices remain very different. Still, it is increasingly possible to think of them as *a* field (as members of *a* family) rather than as disparate fields. The connections between them are strong. The Young British Artists of the 1980s and 1990s, for instance, would (arguably) have achieved nothing like the success they enjoyed if it were not for the attention given them by the media. The shock-horror stories about Tracey Emin's sex life as represented by her work 'My bed' (1998), the revulsion expressed over Damien Hirst's exhibitions of dead animals such as his 'Away from the Flock' (1994), and the theological scandal associated with Chris Ofili's 'The Holy Virgin Mary' (1996), a Madonna adorned with dry elephant dung, ensured that everyone knew about these artists and their work. This in turn raised their profile, increased gallery attendances, built a base for shows of their work to tour internationally, and bumped up sales.

Generally, in fact, art's capacity to inform and influence society depends on the media providing it space to do so. And art gets what can be seen as a disproportionate amount of media coverage, compared with other professions and activities (barring politics and finance). This brings its ideas, stories and discourses to a much wider audience than could have been reached simply through galleries and publishers; thus it is able to comment on society in a way that outstrips its actual social identity.

The mass media, the springboard for this, is itself a field with huge signifying power. Between the news on radio, television and in print, the popular and specialist magazines, television dramas and documentaries, Hollywood film, international and independent movies, the massive music industry and the games and online world, it touches virtually all of us – certainly those living in the First and Second worlds. Its reach is enormous; and, because it is so much a part of our lives and because it repeats stories and ideas over and over, its representations can easily come to seem like truths. This is the 'I heard it on the news: it must be true' syndrome.

But at the same time, it is a very fragmented field. Just to take the case of television, there is remarkable heterogeneity in what can seem to be just one industry. Certainly the commercial channels seem to offer a fairly stable perspective and a steady diet of the same old comedies, dramas and reality shows, but channels such as PBS (US), BBC Four (UK) and SBS (Australia) often show programmes that explore ideologies closely and critically, contest dominant paradigms and even act self-reflexively, critiquing television itself. While CNN or Fox might present news reports that flagrantly support the government of the day, PBS can take a different stance. The practice on the Jim Lehrer News Hour of running, in silence, captioned photographs of troops killed in Iraq or Afghanistan is an explicit, if unstated, criticism both of the government and of the other broadcasters who pay much less attention to the military dead.

THE INFLUENCE OF CONSCIOUSNESS

The cultural – or consciousness – industries are of enormous importance to government because of their capacity to connect with the public. Not only is it the domain where meanings are very actively made and widely disseminated; it is also, according to many commentators, where national life is both manufactured and promoted. This is easily seen in consciously nationalist art, or art produced under contract to the government. The socialist realist works associated with the early Soviet Union, for example, represented Russian workers as strong, healthy and noble in their images and titles. Adolf Strakhov (1896–1979) produced a famous lithograph titled 'Women build socialism' (1926) that presents impressively powerful women at work; a later work of his is titled 'We are the realisation of the plan' (1933–4), a direct statement of the connection between art and government policy. Benjamin Buchloh identifies both fascist and socialist realist painting as 'outright authoritarian styles of representation' (1984: 108), designed to promote bad government. Certainly works produced under and to satisfy those regimes do attempt to produce a perfect match between content and signification: to double the energy of the meaning by performing it in visual and in verbal terms, and in this way to produce the idea/ideal of the nation.

Something similar is evident in much public art. For example, in the Australian national capital, Canberra, is a street bounded on each side by art works that memorialize the various wars in which Australians have fought. At the end of the street is a memorial to the ANZACs, the joint Australian and New Zealand armies that have worked together in a number of theatres of war, a representation themselves of the close relationships between those two countries. It is a doubled memorial: an identical installation is erected on each side of the street, performing what it represents: the idea of very close neighbours, very similar to one another, separated only by a narrow strip (below).

Figure 5.1 The New Zealand Memorial to the Australian and New Zealand Army Corps, ANZAC Parade, Canberra (2001)

The two national flags (almost identical) flutter side by side over a paved area marked with the names of battlefields. On the central block under the great arch is inscribed a poem by New Zealand poet Jenny Bornholdt, which captures in open imagistic phrases something of the relationship represented as existing between these two nations. This poem, reproduced on the next page, manages to combine representations of somewhat contradictory ideas. First, it is carved into stone, which conveys enormous solidity and

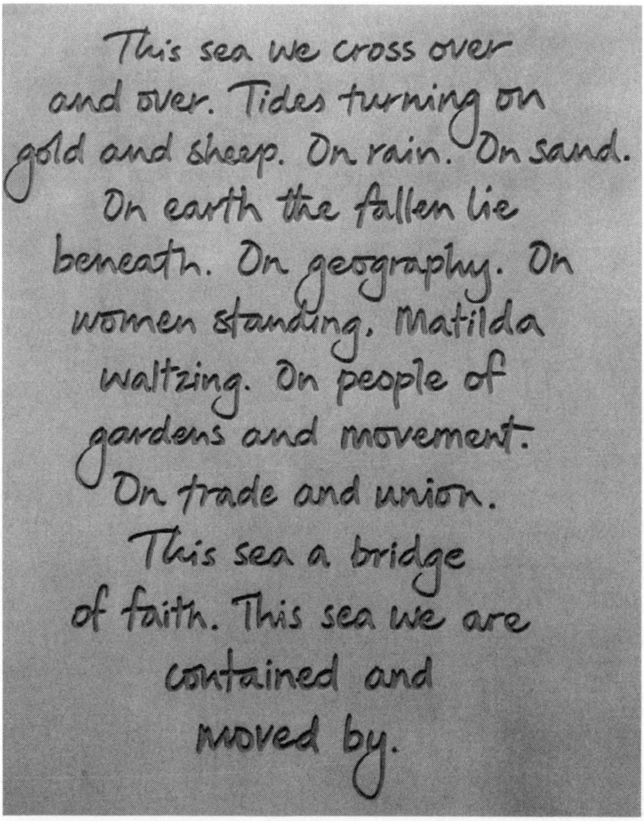

This sea we cross over
and over. Tides turning on
gold and sheep. On rain. On sand.
On earth the fallen lie
beneath. On geography. On
women standing. Matilda
waltzing. On people of
gardens and movement.
On trade and union.
This sea a bridge
of faith. This sea we are
contained and
moved by.

Figure 5.2 'This sea we cross', by New Zealand poet Jenny Bornholdt, inscribed on the New Zealand Memorial, Canberra (2001)

permanence, substantiating the idea of the longevity of nation, and of the relationship between these two nations. It gestures backward to national origins, but also forward to a deep future.

A second move in this text is the representation of everyday life and human presence. The script resembles handwriting, suggesting the presence of an individual making marks for other individuals, and this brings about a personalizing of the poem and its representations. It becomes a friendly act, like the sending of a postcard; and, like a friendly postcard, it says very little about war despite being a war memorial. It is more about 'us', members of the everyday community, getting on with life, as shown in its focus on tides, sheep and goldmines. Only the line 'On earth the fallen lie/beneath' is a direct signifier of war and its cost.

War is about processes of (violent) division. This poem, and indeed the whole installation, is by contrast about tender connection. The sea is a 'bridge of faith'; the sea is one that 'we are contained and moved by'. The pronoun 'we' speaks to both Australians and New Zealanders, to the people here at the bottom of the world, a people representing themselves, and represented, as being committed to peace and primary production. It is a sculptural installation and poem that serves some interests of nationhood, but refuses others. But in the process it makes a very strong claim that there is a people called 'New Zealanders' and another called 'Australians', whose identity is tied to their flags, and found in the stories and icons of their shared and independent histories.

The media takes this process of producing the nation to another level, because of the extent of its reach and the breadth of its content. In fact, for many theorists the national community is largely realized as a direct effect of the mass media. Benedict Anderson, for instance, argues that nations are 'imagined communities' brought into existence in large part by the simultaneity of the mass media. He sheeted this home to 'print capitalism' (Anderson 1983: 42) which produced a daily newspaper in the local language(s), and in the process produced the effect of community among the body of people reading that paper. Up to a few centuries ago, people were more likely to think of themselves as belonging on the one hand to a very local prince or other ruler, and on the other to a universal body, the Church, than to a nation. Print capitalism – for which now we can read mass media products – allowed people to think of themselves as belonging to a very different community – larger than the village, smaller than the Church, and made up of people who shared a language and the narratives of communal identity told in that language.

'We all', for instance, watch the 9 o'clock news, see and hear the same stories, and are told the same ideas from a point of view that drives home the fact that we are 'us', unlike 'everyone else'. And despite the power of genre to structure news in similar ways around the globe, there are local specificities that speak to local issues of identity. For instance, news invariably includes stories of international crisis or disaster, local crises and political events, news about the financial markets, today's weather and weather predictions, and sports news. Local issues emerge in the extent to which overseas news is conveyed, where it is programmed in the whole news bulletin (do we look out, to the global population, or first inward, to ourselves?), and whether international news is only that which would be of interest to local audiences, or is considered of intrinsic interest. Finance news always focuses on how international moves affect the local markets; weather too always starts with local news, though it may extend to present weather stories and predictions on a global level. Sport is a different matter. Though local sport is always important in the reportage, how international and local sports news is told, and what levels of local sports are reported, are markers of what is important to the local community. In the USA, for instance, there is enormous reportage of national US teams and matches; some channels include some overseas sports, usually those that are also important to US audiences; and others again will present state or local sports events at varying levels of professional standing. In Fiji, by contrast to sports news I have seen anywhere else, the results of school sports matches – even primary schools – get coverage on the news. What this suggests is the importance of the local community and all its members, not just those making a living out of their sport. The 'us' in Fiji includes little children, women, men, the chiefs, the ordinary, the military – the whole gamut of society.

The previous chapter explained that difference is an important basis for identity: I am 'me' because I am not 'you'. This extends to a national level, where it becomes 'us' and 'them'. There is considerable representational investment in othering the other, which we see in news bulletins that focus attention on a group of a few million people, treat as secondary the other 7 billion-plus who share the globe, and (currently) represent Muslim people as erratic, volatile, and given to violence. We see this same 'othering' in nineteenth century texts about the peoples of India or Africa, who in European documents were always presented as different from, and less than, the European 'us'. And we see it also in much more contemporary texts. The example below, for instance, could have come out of the writings of any nineteenth century European reflecting on Asia:

> In direct contrast to the fashion for neutral interiors, the new exotica is rich, lush and opulent. Taking its inspiration from the decadent opium dens of 1930s Shanghai, in addition to sybaritic silks from Vietnam, Thailand and Indonesia, contemporary Eastern furnishings mix colour with texture and mysticism with modernity. (Whately 2000: 11)

This is the opening paragraph in a contemporary book about interior decoration that promotes the use of Asian fabrics and *objets d'art* to make one's house more attractive, and more liveable. It does this by relying entirely on what Edward Said named 'Orientalism', the idea of an Orient invented by Europe as 'a place of romance, exotic beings, haunting memories and landscapes, remarkable experiences' (1978: 1). The adjectives in those lines work strictly according to the laws of binary relation. The West is neutral, rational and logical, compared with the 'exotic' East and its opulence, decadence and mysticism. The descriptors are at once appealing (rich, lush) and repulsive (decadent, sybaritic). And, centrally, they are not about Asia; they are about a Western fantasy of Asia as different, as lesser yet attractive, and as always given to disorder and degeneracy (Bhabha 1983: 18).

STATE CULTURE

Orientalism is only one of a number of ways in which the national community is represented and reinforced as different from, and better than, everyone
else. This is not the only way of viewing the effect of the media, though. Guy
Debord suggested in his early work, *Society of Spectacle*, that the media does
more than separate nation from nation; it also wrenches individuals away
from each other and from Nietzsche's 'real truth of nature', plunging them
instead into 'the lie of culture':

> The whole of life of those societies in which modern conditions of production
> prevail presents itself as an immense accumulation of spectacle. All that once was
> directly lived has become mere representation. (1977: 12)

In his perspective, organic relationships with others and, indeed, with communities, are lost, replaced by the 'magical' and entirely empty notion of the
nation. This is a very negative perspective. But even if we take the media at
its more benign face, there are issues worth consideration. For instance, as
Foucault shows in much of his work, it is the responsibility of governments
to manage what people think and how they organize their lives. Given the
capacity of the media to give us tools to think with, it is in the interests of
the state to intervene actively in this sector and manage how these ways of
thinking, ways of organizing society, and ways of managing the relations
between individuals and groups are handled.

It does this by positive and negative means. The positive means include
sponsoring or underwriting particular practices, giving taxation benefits to
media companies, and otherwise shoring up the sector. The negative means
include censorship and other measures of control, such as copyright laws,
anti-racism or anti-sexism laws, and restrictions on the import or export of
media and art products. Here is where the state actively intervenes both to
prescribe and to proscribe representations – to determine what stories may
be told and what images viewed, by whom, and in what ways.

CONTROLLING THE REPRESENTATIONS

Censorship can, of course, be used in a malign way, to control a population and
prevent certain ideas from circulating. This has happened across the globe at
various points in history, and continues to happen now in dictatorships and
other government arrangements where the people have limited political representation. The new legislation produced in the USA, Australia and the UK
following the 11 September 2001 attacks on New York and Washington, for
instance, include considerable powers to limit the circulation of representations.

Censorship also has a more benign aspect, when it is organized to prevent harm. This is the situation where the law 'stands in for' – becomes a ground of representation for – those assumed to be unable to speak for themselves, or to make their own decisions about which representations to view. The protection of children, for instance, is explicit in many censorship acts, along with the protection of all of us from unreasonable offence or hurt. The standard used by most democratic nations is first what would be of offence to a quote/unquote *reasonable adult*; and next what has aesthetic integrity rather than being gratuitous sex or violence.

So within the domain of censorship there are different issues and ideologies at stake, and different outcomes being sought. But at base, it is about representation: what is being said or shown, from what perspective, for what overt and latent outcomes? What do the representations stand for, and what effect might they have on their viewers and on the society at large? Closely linked to censorship is the issue of the politics of representation: the idea that representations can cause real harm. For Kate Bowles, this comes about in one of three ways: 'by risking personal damage to the individual represented; by risking damage by association to the whole class of persons represented; and by risking damage to the person who looks at the image or reads the description' (2002: 78).

Certainly, representations can result in damage. For example, the Dutch filmmaker Theo van Gogh, who was often in the media for his many polemic views, was murdered in 2003 apparently in reaction to his film *Submission*, the story of an arranged marriage in the Muslim community. Obviously his murder was not simply an effect of media representation, but his media presence certainly served to make both him and his views known. There are other levels of damage; libel and slander laws are designed to remedy damage to a person's reputation from being put forward in a negative representation. Damage can be done to someone's peace of mind or sense of self, which is a reason for protecting the vulnerable – children – from frightening or offensive representations.

There is also the issue of representation causing damage to a whole group of people. For example, when women are only, or usually, represented as capable of little more than childcare or food preparation, damage is done to the status of women in society more generally. When Asian people are routinely represented in movies and television shows as unscrupulous villains, it becomes very easy for the public to view all Asians in a negative light. As an example, we can think of Hollywood representations of 'others'. In the 1960s and 1970s, the enemy in Hollywood films was usually represented as someone from the Soviet Union. But by the late 1980s and 1990s, with the collapse of the Soviet Union, a new enemy was needed and now people of 'Middle

Eastern appearance' emerged as the other, the enemy. *True Lies, Executive Decision, Rules of Engagement, The Siege* and many more films provide representations of Muslims as unscrupulous, unreliable and not like us and, arguably, reinforce other negative representations of this community.

IDEOLOGY AND REITERATION

The reason that media products are so influential is first that they consciously make meanings and ways of seeing the world, and second that their images, stories and messages are repeated again and again across many individual shows, products and indeed media. They are the place where ideas are rehearsed and reiterated, to the point that they come to seem obvious, true and inevitable. If you are told the same idea over and over again, then after a while you are likely to be convinced by that idea, consciously or unconsciously. A particularly egregious example of this was **apartheid** South Africa, where in both the concrete and the discursive world, people of colour were treated as secondary. They were not allowed to vote and did not have parliamentary representation; they were not permitted to travel on the same buses, sit on the same park benches, or even be served at the same post office counter, as people of European descent. There were few schools and universities for African students, and they were poorly funded and often quite isolated; housing was substandard and in very restricted locations; their movement was tightly controlled. I could go on ...

This was the lived reality for African people. At the same time, the right of white South Africans to be in the country at all, let alone to rule it, was pretty much unquestioned (in official representations). In media products, the same reality was evident: African people were almost never the main characters in novels or radio plays (there was not at that stage any television produced or shown in South Africa, and the film industry was diminutive). Where they did feature in a media product, it was usually as a servant or a criminal: on the edges both of the story and of society. Because this matched the lived experience, it could easily come to seem a valid and 'true' representation – unless of course the consumer was African, when it would be more likely to seem yet another iteration of abuse and violence.

For the European population, the rehearsed and repeated representation of Africans as servants or violent meant it was difficult to see them in any other way. Should a white South African know a black South African who did not fit those definitions, they would be likely to see that person as an exception to the rule, rather than as an example that the 'rule' was faulty. And black peoples' own perspectives and the representations they would make of themselves and of the culture more generally could not get an airing; at least, not in the public domain where it might have offered a corrective to the dominant representations and what might be called the dominant ideology.

Tim O'Sullivan and colleagues define ideology as 'the practice of reproducing social relations of inequality within the sphere of signification and discourse' (1994: 140); but it is more than just reproducing these social relations of inequality. It is also a matter of coding reality so that the ideas-becoming-ideology seem both natural and inevitable. This is, in effective, what Nietzsche describes in the quote that opens this chapter as 'the lie of culture that poses as if it were the only reality'. Ideology, when it is effective, poses as the only reality. It is not a matter of convincing people or forcing people, but of offering only one reality, and offering it so often, and in so many ways and places, that it seems almost impossible to think in any other way.

The cultural industries are very important in the production and institution of ideologies, because it is the signifying, or symbolic, systems that provide us with the means for understanding the world, and the mediums by which we communicate these understandings and their meanings. This is another, and very important, reason for governments to be interested in managing the cultural industries. Not only do they provide the grounds and the material for the formation of a sense of national community; not only do they need to be regulated to ensure that government-approved ideas circulate; not only do they need to be managed for their economic and social effects such as copyright or vilification, but they also reproduce the relations of power in society. Marx and Engels' very famous axiom is that 'The ideas of the ruling class are in every epoch the ruling ideas' (1976 [c.1845]: 67) and, given the importance of the cultural industries in transmitting ideas, we can safely argue that to a large extent the cultural industries promote ideas and ideologies that suit the interests of the 'ruling class' in the discourses they promote, and in what they treat as important and valuable. The cultural industries, as Adorno points out (1991), typically do not impose ideas on people, but rather present a very limited range of possible ideas.

THREE WARS

To see this more clearly, let's consider three movies about America at war. The first, *Red Dawn* (1984), represents what might happen if the USA were invaded by an enemy. The blurb describes it thus:

> *Red Dawn* opens with one of the most shocking scenes ever filmed; on a peaceful morning, through the windows of a high school classroom, students see paratroopers land on the varsity football field: the invasion of the United States has begun!

It is difficult for someone not American, and/or someone not living in the 1980s, to be able to conceive of this as 'one of the most shocking scenes ever filmed'. But if the writer's starting point is American exceptionalism (the belief that the USA is different from all other nations, and has a special role to play) and manifest destiny (the belief that the USA has a right and a destiny to expand territorially), then it does become a shocking scene. The central idea, that it is shocking and indeed morally wrong to invade America, is reiterated throughout the movie. The invaders are Russian, Cuban and Latin American Communists who take over a vast area of the continental USA, imprison and torment the civilians, and summarily execute people who offer any resistance – or simply to make a point.

The story is focalized through two football-playing, gun-toting, missile-humping, traitor-killing, hell-raising, commie-bashing, all-American brothers played by (a very young) Patrick Swayze and Charlie Sheen. Shown from a different perspective, they could seem thoroughly obnoxious, racist, sexist, ignorant thugs. But in the context of this film, they are difficult but admirable young men: brave, tough and loyal. Their skills in football, shooting and survivalism are the key points that allow the band of friends to survive through most of the movie – and more than survive. Rather than keeping their heads down, they form a guerilla band and attack the invaders at every point, with remarkable success.

The idea of American values is rehearsed throughout, even in this aspect – the boys call their militia group by the same name as their school football team, the Wolverines, drawing an obvious parallel between American football and war, but also a parallel between American football and the value of freedom. An example of this reiterated narrative is a scene where the invaders are about to initiate a mass execution of civilians. A number of people – including the brothers' father – are lined up, waiting for the bullets. Rather than showing panic or stoicism, the townspeople break into an impromptu (and off-key) version of 'America the Beautiful', a display of courage, patriotism and resistance that is ended only by the invaders' bullets.

Red Dawn could double as a movie sponsored by the National Rifle Association (NRA) and the militia movement. The logic is that if the civilians are armed, they can defend their nation against a sneak attack by evil invaders. It could also double as a movie sponsored by the Men's Movement. The fathers and other townsmen captured by the invaders tend to wear militia style moustaches and to own arsenals of weapons. The mothers are invisible, by and large, and the two female characters, the sisters who join the young rebels, are presented to the boys not as people but as their grandfather's 'heirlooms'. The enemy are bad Russians and Cubans, along with a rather more sympathetic Latin American who understands what it means to be a partisan. It is difficult to read this movie 'straight' (in terms of its own values) from the vantage of 20-plus years, and knowing what the USA has done in terms of international relationships – invading Vietnam, for instance, or Granada, or Iraq. But the logic of the film and all the techniques of representation are designed to reiterate and reinforce American virtue, and the virtue of arms.

Compare this with a film released nearly two decades later. *The Sum of All Fears* (2002) is another movie imbued with Cold War tensions, though it is set 13 years after the collapse of the Soviet Union. This does not diminish the tension invoked by the film. The title alone indicates its central message – it is the sum of *all* fears. Whose fears these might be, or who is invoked by the title, is not made particularly clear. Unlike *Red Dawn*, which is comfortably a them-and-us movie, structured in terms of binary logic, *All Fears* raises the spectre of the final nuclear holocaust – the sum of fear for everyone on the planet. At the same time, the old Soviets are definitely the bad guys. Their president is reasonable – and more than reasonable; he is urbane. But then, he was educated abroad and presumably has taken on some aspects of Western values.

The film begins by setting the scenario: as the opening credits roll, we are taken to the Yom Kippur War of 1973 when Egypt and Syria attacked Israel. We observe an Israeli pilot, armed with a nuclear missile, being shot down, and then leap 29 years into the future, and from the Middle East to middle America. The missile has been found by a herdsman, and sold to European right wingers, ruthless and lacking in human qualities, who are determined to undermine new Russia and launch an attack on the USA. They manage to launch the missile at a sports event in America, causing huge destruction and bringing the American leadership to the point of launching reprisal attacks on Russia.

The film operates with the same sort of material as *Red Dawn*: America is a fine nation being unfairly attacked, and now must be defended with all force. But it is considerably more subtle in its ideological framework. Where *Red Dawn* fails to look beyond the US borders, *All Fears* moves easily across the globe; where *Red Dawn* can find positive qualities only in Americans (bar the glimmer of humanity we see in the Latin American ex-partisan), *All Fears* shows the American leadership as flawed, and offers a sympathetic portrayal of at least some Europeans. However, the idea that America is, first, in charge of the world and second, not to be subject to violence, is played out throughout the film. In one scene, for instance, the Russian president snaps at the Americans that 'Chechnya is none of your concern'. Morgan Freeman, who plays the CIA director, responds, 'Stability is our concern. Peace in Chechnya is our concern'; or, to read it in another way, 'You may be a sovereign state, but you are behaving badly, and America has the right and the responsibility to intervene'.

It also shows an America very different from how the current administration has been operating. There is a sort of apologia happening throughout the representations made of American and geopolitical relations, because the USA only intervenes to prevent 'the sum of all fears', and to protect those genuinely being abused. Ben Affleck's Dr Ryan, the CIA expert, is reasonable, sophisticated and 'internationalized': he speaks a number of Eastern European languages with complete aplomb. In one scene, for instance, he rescues a CIA operative by speaking to the guards in their own language, and the operative says to him, 'You speak Ukrainian?', in some surprise. 'Yeah,' says Ryan, 'You don't?' This casual assumption that US operatives actually connect, converse and engage effectively with the rest of the world is charming, and goes some way to validate US interventionism. Compare this with the current situation, where as Hendrik Hertzberg writes, of the 1,000 US embassy staffers in Iraq, only six are fluent speakers of Arabic, with another 27 who are not fluent speakers. He goes on to state, in parentheses, '(fifty-five Arabic language specialists have been cashiered from the military for being gay)' (2006: 34).

By the end of the film, the Americans have overcome their internal dissent and their external enemies. They are back in the saddle, and back on-side with their international allies. Theirs has been an approach committed to global accord under the benign oversight of the USA, rather than the sort of Godzilla-like blundering we have observed over the past years in the Middle Eastern engagements or the American triumphalism of *Red Dawn*. The film comes to a close after a speech made by the US president (James Cromwell), who says, 'There is no more fitting memorial for those who perished in this tragedy than the steps we have taken this week toward a multinational campaign to root out and eliminate weapons of mass destruction.' This sense that America can be a member, rather than a controller, of the global family is a long way from *Red Dawn*'s view of the world.

The third film is a documentary made by Australian artist George Gittoes on the US war in Iraq. *Soundtrack to War* (2004) is a series of interviews – or chats, really – between Gittoes (who is always behind the camera, present only as a voice) and US troops about their musical preferences, and what music helps them get through the day. Music is a useful vehicle for this visual essay. It allows the service people to speak perhaps more openly than other topics might, about their anxieties and aspirations: 'War is heavy metal', says one respondent, against a background of shelling and heavy metal music, a throbbing, driving, painful sound.

Their recounting of their tastes, and singing of their favourite songs, both individualizes and humanizes the soldiers. As a documentary rather than a fiction film, the representations are both more and less evident. Gittoes presents in some ways as a neutral observer, interested only in what the servicemen and -women have to say, but the timing of scenes, the angle of shot, the objects that come under the camera's scrutiny, and the editorial voice over all go to present a particular view of this moment in history. It is deeply sympathetic to the troops, but rather than supporting the American action, it shows a beleaguered group of (mostly) young people in a staggeringly difficult situation, separated from their own family and home, and equally separated from the people of Iraq. They are locked away in the Green Zone except when they are locked away in armoured vehicles, travelling in some terror through hostile streets.

Gittoes, unlike the American military, is able to move about in Baghdad proper, and interviews a number of Iraqis about their taste in music – and, inevitably, about the effects of the war. There is a group of young Iraqi musicians who love heavy metal, something forbidden in their culture. They are caught between the threat of being discovered playing metal by their community, killed by Americans, or caught in a random bombing in the streets of Baghdad. Their response is to play more music, though they talk openly about their lack of hope for a future. Gittoes also interviews an older group of Iraqi musicians who are great fans of the Bee Gees. They perform a cover of the Bee Gee's song 'New York Mining Disaster' ('Have you seen my wife Mr Jones?/Do you know what it's like on the outside?'), a profoundly disturbing juxtaposition of a gentle pop song with a horrific war, of a Western mining disaster with their entrapment in these unremittingly violent streets.

'War isn't political, when you're in it … it's just survival', says Gittoes in the director's commentary – a line that is something of a coda for the whole film. But of course it is political – at an individual and a national level. What they are all doing in Iraq comes up in virtually every interview, and in virtually every interview a double answer is given. Although a handful of the service people seem to genuinely believe in what they are doing, and to hold to a *Red Dawn* notion of American values or a *Sum of All Fears* notion of America's role in the world, most of them are just making a living, and getting by. For example, Gittoes interviews Janelle, a young mechanic-cum-musician who sings a piece she has written about her sense of war. He asks, 'What's a beautiful, talented young lady like you doing in the army?' and she grins, and says 'Serving my country'. This answer – the textbook response – is in fact only a joke. She bursts into helpless laughter, and so do the young men working alongside her, because her line is the official answer that no one believes, or that no one can take seriously.

Gittoes finds something similar among virtually all the people who make it to the final cut of the movie: their concerns are not American politics, or saving the world for democracy. Rather, they want to talk about their music, about friends who have been killed, their family back home, how long it is since they've had sex, and how much they miss the small everyday things of peacetime life. The ordinariness of human beings even in extraordinary circumstances, and the similarities between us that are obscured by the binary logic of us/them, are made manifest in this documentary: it is a representation of the world where ordinary people are just trying to get by, despite the violence of official politics: a gentle but still probing criticism of both American and Iraqi leadership. What this suggests is that cultural products do not tell just one story, or represent just one point of view. Other perspectives are always likely to slip in, even in the apparently most clearcut and direct ideological statement.

OVER TO ART

Let me shift focus now to art-proper, the domain in which purely symbolic objects are produced, those obedient to aesthetic rather than economic or communicative logic. Much is written about art's lack of social investment, and incapacity to deliver representations that have any effect – especially when compared with the sheer power of the mass media. But this is not the only way to look at it. For example, South African photographer David Goldblatt worked for some years as a journalist and, according to the didactic panels at the Tate Modern (July 2004), he set out to record the effects of apartheid, but lost heart in his ability to change the situation. He shifted to art and sought to evoke, and elucidate, rather than just show news reportage of the state of affairs. In this he reverses the usual hierarchy of impact, where news has greater representational power than 'mere art'.

Nonetheless, art is often considered a special case when it comes to representation because it focuses principally on form. Indeed, art is as much about *presentation* as about *re*presentation: artworks may or may not (re)present an absent referent, but they certainly do present themselves *as* image. In addition, they perform some of the work of subjectivity because an image will 'constitute the person who looks at it as the looking subject' (Chartier 1997: 91). It need not do anything more than this; it need not refer to anything beyond itself; and hence it need not rely on the metaphysics of presence to move or connect with its viewers.

Nonetheless, in many works it is possible to detect a yearning for presence. The poet Rainer Maria Rilke, for instance, wrote on the manuscript of his *Duino Elegies* (1924):

> Happy are those who know:
> Behind all words, the unsayable stands;

And from that source alone, the infinite
Crosses over to gladness, and to us –
Free of our bridges,
Built with the stone of distinctions;
So that always, within each delight,
We gaze at what is purely single and joined. (cited Hirshfield 1997: 56)

The *Duino Elegies* do, generally, tease out Rilke's sense of what can only be felt, can never be said, and what for him lies behind all representation – the 'unsayable' that nonetheless *is*. The unsayable is our route to 'gladness', 'freedom', and at the same time a perfect unity, 'purely single and joined'. It is paradoxical, impossible, but it is also what can be found at the heart of most religions and philosophies of presence: that out there, if you have the right attitude or relation or openness, the unsayable, infinite gladness will become available to you too.

Despite the move in twentieth century art towards abstraction and away from mimesis, towards irony and away from Rilke, art does not necessarily provide a way out of representation, or an alternative to that mode:

art is not a representation of the world, because in art presentation stands out as the dominant pole. However, representation does not disappear, the aesthetic value of art is depending on a dynamic equilibrium between representation and presentation. (Østergård 1996: 109, n3)

The metaphysics of presence, and the need to frame both thoughts and feelings, remain in art. The tension between representation and presentation is perhaps most evident in what are often called representational works: a portrait of someone, for instance, or a landscape or still life. Such works are not supposed to be realistic versions of the subject, or direct reflections – a camera could achieve that. But they are supposed to capture *something*; perhaps the personality or character of the sitter, perhaps the feeling of the landscape, or the texture of the objects in a still life. They combine presentation and representation in that dynamic manner.

The work shown on p.124 is by Japanese Australian artist Chaco Kato. It is a section of her drawing-by-sewing called 'In a rainy room' (2003). It is a representational work; it shows recognizable things: a spider's web, small girls, raindrops, and some enormous nets. It is not really representational though, because it contains unlikely or impossible, and certainly unsettling, juxtapositions. Why is rain falling, and why is a large thistle growing inside the house? That would normally be a sign of decay, deterioration, perhaps the effects of war or a massive natural catastrophe – and yet the little girls seem perfectly relaxed, even interested in their surroundings. The nets are unexpected – and provoke the question, 'what are they trying to catch?' Their

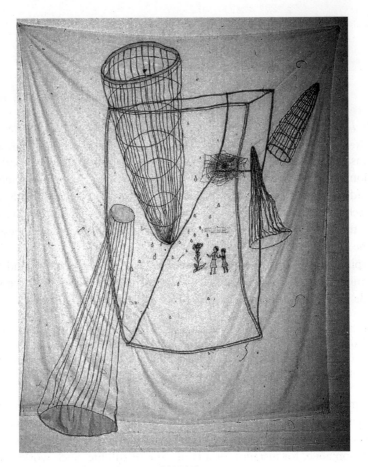

Figure 5.3 C. Kato, 'In a rainy room' (2003)

target must be the little girls, who are equally threatened by the web that hovers over them, in gigantic proportions, and yet seem perfectly content, even delighted. Viewing this and other works in the same show was a profoundly unsettling experience, not because they are overtly 'about', say, war, or catastrophe, but because they show the world from an unexpected angle, and because they raise questions but offer no answers. The images work in a 'dynamic' tension between presentation and representation.

Even more elusive and abstracted works still retain some connection with content; they are not just colour, movement or sound. They are, obviously, concerned more with presentation than with representation but, as Østergård suggests, it is not as simple as that. Abstract, non-representational works rarely make themselves entirely available to the viewer's imagination to come up with any meaning they like. Instead, exhibitions and catalogues provide artist notes, titles and didactics that explain to viewers what they are seeing. Another work by Chaco Kato, 'Migration' (from the show *Migration*, Melbourne 2001), breaks with the impulse to record in lines what can be seen. It is not representational because there is little or no substitution, or delegation of presence. The work is an installation of stones, string and glass bubbles which are not standing in for, or being substituted for: the stones are themselves; the glass bubbles are themselves (below). But for Kato, and as explained in the accompanying catalogue essay, the installation is a statement about the difficulty of hanging on

Figure 5.4 C. Kato, 'Migration' (2001)

to one's identity, one's language, and one's connections to the past in a new environment that is often hostile to immigrants. The strings looping among the objects express her belief in the interconnectedness of everyone. The etched teardrops have the fragility and scarring that mark the migrant, the refugee, and the exile. Each stone pertains to one of the people she interviewed while producing work for the show, and is etched with the name of their father or mother, or with their favourite word in their own language and script – a reminder that as long as those who love us remain, or our words remain, we too remain. So Kant may be correct, and logic may have little or nothing to do with the rules of feeling. But no viewer's response can be entirely idiosyncratic and personal. Each person will bring to the viewing, and hence the effect of such a work, those things provided them by additional information and by their personal history. Each of these will be embedded in a socio-historical context that delimits what they can see, know, and feel.

WHAT PIPE?

Perhaps the apogee of the non- or anti-representationalist attitude in art is found in Rene Magritte's famous work 'The treason of images' (1929).[1] It is more commonly known by the phrase written across the painting, 'Ceci n'est pas une pipe' [this is not a pipe]. The work simultaneously points to the problem of representation – that a symbol cannot deliver presence – and the doubling of representation – the pipe is clearly 'a' pipe, in that anyone looking at it would name it such. Yet it is not; it is only a representation. As Foucault points out, it is an ambiguous drawing (or drawings, since there is a pipe on a canvas within the painting); it is not clear whether Magritte is disclaiming the meta-pipe or the embedded drawing of a pipe as not-pipe. And of course neither of the images is a pipe; each is a drawing, a representation, and not of just any pipe, but of 'an ideal pipe – simple notion or fantasy of a pipe' (1983: 16). There is no true pipe to which the images refer – the 'true' pipe is just 'a pipe dream' (ibid). The painting inscribed 'This is not a pipe' is a painting of a pipe (with a painting of a pipe), which produces a mixed dependency on idea, image and word; and, of course, on the referent itself.

This work has attracted considerable attention from theorists and from other artists. For Eric Rauth it can be read as 'an iconic subversion of the reassuring borders between word and image, and even as a travesty of Jesus' pronouncement *Hoc est corpus meum* [this is my body] at the Last Supper' (2002: 33). That is to say, it is a form of representation that relies on the icon rather than the symbol; that tends towards resemblance rather than symbolic representation; and yet drops into that material an entirely symbolic statement that upsets any comfortable viewing of the work as 'just a painting' of a pipe. And it does it in the interests of disturbing the rules of meaning. As Rauth goes on to write:

> In transubstantiation we must ignore the evidence of the eyes (the visible wafer) in favor of the statement, while in Magritte's picture we must ignore the statement in favor of the evidence of the eyes (itself only an optical illusion and not a real presence). (2002: 39, n23)

Like much of the work produced in the art world, Magritte's painting takes seriously the claims of both resemblance and representation, and speaks back to those concepts. It has been appropriated by many artists to carry the ideas a little further. For instance, the Tate Modern boasts a very ordinary rubbish bin, on the edge of the lawn outside the museum and facing the Thames,

---

[1] Called, in some translations, 'The betrayal of images'; an image can be seen at http://www.magrittefoundation.org/EN/foundation.html

which proclaims 'This is not a photo opportunity'. This very self-conscious bit of graffiti/public art is quoting Magritte, and also having a bit of fun at the expense of all tourists and consumers of art whose intention is to capture some souvenir of their moment, to retain the truth of presence – both the physical objects and location, and the historical presence of their visit to the Tate. It is also, perhaps, teasing the salacious interest of those captivated by the invitation to 'spank me' at the bottom of the bin – but that's another issue.

The point in this is that art is not simply representative or simply aesthetic; it is also a localized, situated and temporal form of communication and knowledge. Work we read as representational is so primarily because of contemporary codes that tell us it 'looks real'. A photographic portrait of a person, for instance, looks like that person only in contingent terms, only because in our culture we have particular norms for resemblance and for representation.

Figure 5.5 'This is not a photo opportunity': graffiti on rubbish bin at the Tate Modern, London (2004)

The discussion about whether particular works of art make 'true' representations, or are abstractions, or are 'realistic' is very much tied to historical time and to contemporary debates in art, and to the availability of forms of technology. Kress and van Leeuwen describe the way in which, over the past decades, 'realism' changed from being a description of whether a visual representation *looked like* its subject: whether it was 'naturalistic'. In the photographic world, up till the mid-twentieth century, a 'good' – which is to say, a naturalistic or mimetic – portrait of someone would almost always be in black-and-white. But:

> For us, now, as commonsense viewers, everyday members of society at large, the defining technology is that of 35mm colour photography. And the relatively recent change from the dominance of black and white to the dominance of colour in many domains of visual communication shows how quickly these histories develop, and how closely they are related to technological change. (Kress and van Leeuwen 1996: 163)

Which is to say, something appears to be real, mimetic, or abstract on the basis of the cultural contexts, the dominant codes of reading, the ideological frameworks operating at that time, and the range of technologies available to viewers.

CONCLUSION

Barthes writes:

> in theater, in cinema, in traditional literature, things are always seen *from somewhere*; this is the geometric basis of representation: there must be a fetishistic subject in order to project this tableau. The point of origin is always the Law: law of society, law of struggle, law of meaning. (1985: 96)

Certainly it is possible to view art and the mass media – including television, cinema, theatre, advertisements and new media products – as providing a point from which to see: a point that lays down the law of seeing, the 'law of society'. It is a sector with enormous reach into society, with enormous capacity to make real only particular and limited points of view. But because it is filled with and consumed by people in all their particularities, it never gives only one point of view. As fast as one aspect of the sector is shoring up the conservative view, for instance, another is urging radical change; one part encourages capitalism, another encourages people to move towards a new counter-cultural life; one side makes the emptiness and the game of representation very transparent, and another presents its products as though they are windows onto reality. It is not a fixed or monolithic sector; so it can be the place where both radical change and deep consolation are made available, and where the complexities and perplexities of being both subject of representation and living body can be understood and accommodated. It is also a site where the politics, and the ethics, of being human are constantly tested; and this is the topic of the final chapter.

Conclusion: Representation and ethics – the problem of the gap

J.M. Coetzee's Booker Prize-winning novel, *The Life and Times of Michael K*, raises the problem of the gap between representation and reality, and the effects that gap can have on the lived experience of individuals. It recounts the story of Michael K, a rather simple gardener from Cape Town, who leaves the city in a time of emergency and finds himself alone on the farm where his mother grew up. Cut off from everyone by his incapacity to understand other's representations or to make effective representations himself, he hides away in the country, as far as possible avoiding other people, and reducing himself to little more than bare life. The quote below comes from a scene where, while in hiding, he observes a group of guerillas arrive at the farm where he is living:

> K knew that he would not crawl out and stand up and cross from darkness into fire-light to announce himself. He even knew the reason why: because enough men had gone off to war saying the time for gardening was when the war was over; whereas there must be men to stay behind and keep gardening alive, or at least the idea of gardening; because once that cord was broken, the earth would grow hard and forget her children. That was why. ... Between this reason and the truth that he would never announce himself, however, lay a gap wider than the distance separating him from the firelight. Always, when he tried to explain himself to himself, there remained a gap, a hole, a darkness before which his understanding baulked, into which it was useless to pour words. The words were eaten up, the gap remained. His was always a story with a hole in it: a wrong story, always wrong. (1983: 150–1)

There are several gaps suggested in these lines. One is the space between ideology and existence – war versus gardening. Another is the space between two different values systems – political and existential ('the idea of gardening'; the human connection with the planet). And yet another, the main one, is the gap between story and experience. He cannot find a way through the space between himself, a subject who has fallen out of representation, and everyone else, the bearers of political identity. Consequently narrative – or discourse – is insufficient for him: 'His was always a story with a hole in it'.

This 'story with a hole', the space between representation and existence, is the subject of this chapter. We have discussed in the earlier chapters the propensity of representation to constitute both us as subjects and the world in which we live. It is a system of production that is endlessly tolerant, in that it accommodates a vast range of often contradictory 'truths', but also entirely intolerant, because individuals must buy in to the system to have a recognizable social existence, and many people and groups of people can barely do so: they do not meet its criteria. What this implies is that something utterly central to representation is social identity, and that beyond its logics, its techniques and its history is the story of how it is used to make social reality, and how we might analyse the frameworks it sets around our world.

Mikhail Bakhtin explains this with reference to language, writing:

Discourse lives, as it were, beyond itself, in a living impulse toward the object; if we detach ourselves completely from this impulse all we have left is the naked corpse of the word, from which we can learn nothing at all about the social situation or the fate of a given word in life. (1981: 292)

Similarly, to study representation as an idea or thing, rather than as a process in use, leaves the analyst with little but 'the naked corpse' of representation. This raises the question of representation as a process: what can our understandings of representation permit? How can knowledge of its workings, be used to craft a better situation for people?

Bakhtin again stresses the importance of building understandings of the generative structures in which we live, pointing out that 'the better a person understands the degree to which he is externally determined, the closer he comes to understanding and exercising his own freedom' (1981: 139). 'Freedom' itself is, of course, only a representation, but one with enormous capacity to drive discourse, and one that carries an enormous weight of value. In this chapter I will explore the idea of being able to think through the limitations imposed by the terms of representation at any given point in history and culture, and to strive to stretch the boundaries of society so that individuals can more easily be accommodated, and on terms of greater equity. After all, as Gilles Deleuze writes, 'Representation no longer exists; there's only action – theoretical action and practical action which serve as relays and form networks' (1972: 206–7).

ACTION OR SIMULATION?

We can read this as stating that the problem with representation is that it does not provide presence, only abstractions. Since all human action involves something concrete, this means there is a gap between how we articulate a situation or problem – an event – and how we address it. The event comes to one's attention in ephemeral or amorphous form – as a representation. To attend to it, we must perceive it as a concrete thing, and take concrete action – perform an act that addresses the event. And then that act itself will take on meaning *as* representation. It will add to the weight of empty signification that makes our reality for us.

The emptiness of representation is of signal importance here, because it designates a space in which there is some elbow room. On the one hand we have concrete reality which, as I have discussed in earlier chapters, cannot be contained in any system of representation. On the other we have representation itself, that which is not real, and yet is much more 'real' to us – because it is both accessible and the terms of access – than the 'real world'.

The theorist perhaps most closely associated with this gap, this impossible connection between reality and representation, is Jean Baudrillard. In his famous book *Simulations* (1983) he lays out his theory of this problem, and describes the absence of any 'natural' connection between referent and representation. What this means, for Baudrillard, is what we have seen in earlier chapters: that no sign means in and of itself, or connects directly with any 'real' thing, but rather has meaning only in context – only in relation to other signs, and not to reality (1983: 32). Central to this, he writes, is that the real does not come first, for us. We do not look at the world 'out there' and come up with representations that frame what we see. Rather, the representations come first – what he terms 'the precession of the simulacrum' – and these representations 'produce' the world for us (1983: 3). Arguably the technological developments over the past years have made this increasingly relevent. As Baudrillard again (and more recently) writes, 'Modern technologies ... are no longer so much extensions of man, as McLuhan used to say, but human beings are now becoming rather, a kind of extension of the logistical system' (2001: 289). Which is to say, the context itself precedes our experience of that context.

This is a well-worked field. Ludwig Wittgenstein, for instance, wrote 'we see it as we interpret it' (1958: 193); and for Jean-Luc Nancy, it is 'not a world nor the world that takes on figure, but the figure that makes world' (1993: 29). For philosophers generally, meaning is not actuality; it is simply a matter of how signs are juxtaposed, and so 'truth, reference and objective causes have ceased to exist' (Baudrillard 1983: 6). Reality itself does not exist (or rather, does not exist for us outside the domain of representation): 'for reality is a principle, and it is this principle that is lost' (Baudrillard 2002: 28). This is not to suggest that there is nothing *in fact* outside the sign; but that human beings are incapable of experiencing that 'outside'. We both experience, and anticipate our experiences, through mediated forms: through the telling of other experiences, through the arguments presented in the mass media, and through contemporary ways of making sense. These are the simulacra that 'precede' the real and make it available to us, only as mediation. He writes that this is the case even for acts of violence:

> all hold-ups, hijacks and the like are now as it were simulation hold-ups, in the sense that they are inscribed in advance in the decoding and orchestration rituals of the media, anticipated in their mode of presentation and possible consequences. (1983: 198)

Not everyone would share this perspective; for most commentators, it seems, terrorism always comes unanticipated. Certainly I, and most people, were surprised by the events of 11 September 2001 – who could have anticipated that? And yet the media very quickly found ways of delimiting it, of reducing it to a spectacle, and of bringing it into a sense-making structure (*we stand for freedom; they hate our freedom; therefore they attack us*). This is not, again, to suggest that something singular did not happen on 11 September. Derrida also commented on that attack, though he did not go as far as Baudrillard in separating the event from its representation. For Derrida:

> The 'impression' [of the event] cannot be dissociated from all the affects, interpretations, and rhetoric that have at once reflected, communicated, and 'globalized' it, from everything that also and first of all formed, produced, and made it possible. The 'impression' thus resembles 'the very thing' that produced it. Even if the so-called thing cannot be reduced to it. Even if, therefore, the event itself cannot be reduced to it. The event is made up of the 'thing' itself (that which happens or comes) and the impression (itself at once 'spontaneous' and 'controlled') that is given, left, or made by the so-called 'thing'. (2003: 88–9)

The event resembles its representation; the representation resembles the event; they are not identical with each other but they exist for us hand in hand. The representation allows us to make (some) sense of what is going on, but we can never really experience it in all its fullness because it belongs in the realm of reality, that which is always other to us, the subjects of representation. The point here is Deleuze's point, quoted earlier: that once we understand the terms of representation, our task is to take theoretical and practical action. What we choose to do, and why, is something that can only be answered by contemplating the question of ethics.

REPRESENTING THE WRONG

For many people of the later twentieth and twenty-first centuries, the most egregious example of 'wrong' theoretical and practical action, of negative relays, is found in Nazi Germany. Its leaders are represented in history (as indeed they should be) as among the very worst. 'We all' know that Hitler was a monster, the SS were demons, the Goebbels were icy brutes, and so on. Fair enough. And most of the narratives we have of the Second World War, and especially of the Nazi management of Germany and Europe, set those people in parentheses as a bizarre and appalling aberration of history – as people who are not like us, as people who do and think things 'we' would never do or think. But this is faulty representation on our part: it ignores the material experience of all of history, and the capacity of human beings to craft actions and networks that lead only to the grave. It is not really an aberration; it is business as usual, only cranked up a few notches.

The movie *Downfall* (2004) teases out this problem of human being and ethical interactions because its representation of those (non-)people is as *people*. We may not like them, we certainly wouldn't want to spend much time with them, but fundamentally they are shown to be of the same order as the rest of the human race. *Downfall* is focalized through Hilter's young secretary, Traudl Junge. Through her eyes we see the German officers, both Nazi and army, trying to bring some reason into an insane world: ordinary people struggling with ordinary concerns in an extraordinary world. We see the SS physician attempting to maintain conventional medical ethics while his Führer is seeking only death for all. We see Magda Goebbels torn between her fanatical passion for National Socialism and her desire for her children to have a future (of course, she chooses against the future). Hitler himself is insanely vicious, and yet sweet and considerate towards Traudl, who says, 'In private he can be such a caring person. But then he says such … brutal things'. In short, we see members of the Third Reich as human beings, doing a lot of very ordinary, very human things: being complicit, or courageous, cowed or pragmatic, seeking their own benefit or concerned for their nation … and so on. It is a representation of that time in history and that set of human beings that does not shed new light on the history itself – does not act in any way as an apologia – but reminds us that in the same situation, we would probably behave in just the same way.

Much of the work of science, philosophy and religion is dedicated to exploring how we can go so wrong; and how to avoid it in the future. And yet 'wrong' is itself a representation; as *Downfall* shows, for the Nazis and for many ordinary Germans it was a matter first of doing the 'right thing' (however appalling that might seem now), and then of trying to survive. There really isn't right or wrong; only ways of framing actions and events, and of measuring them against standards that are themselves never stable.

ETHICAL LIVING

Michel de Certeau addresses this problem of how to live ethically in a context where there are no real measures. He argues that knowledge, and understandings of knowledge and how it works, are starting points. In our era the point of knowledge is, Certeau writes, 'to produce a more humane world' (1986: 199). And we can start doing so by examining the terms and conditions of knowledge, and especially of what is represented as the truth of being. Ethics is, for Certeau, that which 'defines a distance between what is and what ought to be. This distance designates a space where we have something to do' (1986: 199). Rosalyn Diprose too defines ethics as a 'somewhere' that is an action. She points out that the term 'ethics':

> is derived from the Greek word *ethos*, meaning dwelling, or habitat – the place to which one returns. ... To belong to, and project out from an *ethos* is to take up a position in relation to others. (1991: 65)

Finding the space, and finding how to take action in and from that space, is the starting point for ethics. We can see here shades of Deleuze's insistence that it is action, and not representation, that matters. Representation makes our context, but we ought not simply float along in its sea. Instead, we should understand theoretically and practically what is going on, and find the space where there is 'something to do'.

This is not, of course, a clear or direct path. As with everything human beings do, it is fraught with competing ideologies, competing priorities, and the impossibility of establishing just how things are and therefore what there is 'to do'. The ethical domain is no more clear or complete than any other aspect of representation – it too is marked always by difference and deferral. The person who institutes a break with the dominant ideology, who claims the ethical responsibility to do things differently, is likely to slip into the metaphysics of presence and into the game of power, simply in order to get those things done. As Certeau again writes, what we tend to do in our effort to get things done is to claim that we are the ones who see things 'right'; who have a clearer connection to the 'real' world (1986: 203). In the interests of 'telling it like it is' and therefore seeking ways of ameliorating human suffering or inequity, we are likely to claim that we ourselves have the only 'right' way of doing things, the only 'true' handle on things, and that we therefore have the right to tell other people what to do: much as Hitler, presumably, thought about his own sense of the world.

Representation is always both performative and citational: it always acts – or brings things into being – as well as naming those things; it always allows meaning to be made, yet prevents it from being made (in any 'real' sense). It is the material we use to construct society, social realities and relations of power, but:

> essentially it is an open game where closure is never achieved and where there is always some room for contestation of given representations – even if that room may in some circumstances be severely, and too, limited. (Thomassen 2006)

Representation is, therefore, crafted over a void, and yet is potent with authority because people see it as actuality, or as that which is capable of delivering presence.

REPRESENTATION AND RIGHTS

This can be exemplified by discussing how the ideas of representation, ethics and human being converge and crash at the point of 'human rights'. Human rights law and logic depend on there being a clear idea of what a human is. As we saw in Chapter 3, human beings exist as they do because systems of representation provide the simulacra that precedes the real of lived being. It makes us human, and different from all the rest of reality. But it also makes us separate from ourselves, internally divided. In Chapter 4 we saw that individuals become 'humans', 'like us', when they are represented in political terms, because they then belong to a community and can take up political life. In Chapter 5 I discussed Benedict Anderson's notion that nationalism is an idea that comes into being only through the imaginary – for instance through representations made in the mass media in which 'we all' (the members of a nation) recognize ourselves and one another. Michael Ignatieff (1994) takes this a step further, pointing out that nations are not just ideas produced as actuality, because they are grounded on ties of blood, common history and tradition, or the simultaneity of the media. Rather, nations are grounded on that super-representational site, law. It is the legal-juridicial framework that both represents and constitutes a nation-state, and hence confines the possibilities of being that are enjoyed by its citizens.

Human beings are, thus, the products of representation across a number of domains, and not the result of reality (in reality we would, presumably, be simply living organisms, not different in kind from algae and antelope). Human rights law is designed to recognize us in our particularity, *as* humans, as those beings made a little lower than the angels, and owed a range of rights and freedoms. But it is directed not at me and you, at particular individuals, but at 'humanity' (Slaughter 1997: 7). Here is its big problem. Humanity does not exist; only 'you' and 'I' exist. Humanity is only an abstraction, an empty signifier, that has to be filled with meaning by those capable of saying who counts as part of 'humanity', and who is thus deserving of protection under the law.

The Universal Declaration of Human Rights was proclaimed and adopted in 1948 largely in response to the horrors of the Second World War, in an attempt to suture the gap between Us and Them. It operates under the premise that everyone who is human has equal access to rights. But it overlooks the contradictions that are the starting point for any interaction between human beings, or between states. In its attempt to craft one single community – humankind – it forgets the issues of inclusion and exclusion on which all communities are built. It is not a concrete act, but a representation.

It is also a representation with a long history, and very wide general acceptance. Micheline Ishay traces the enactment of rights in law from the Code of Hammurabi to the US Patriot Act, and shows just how fundamental is the universalist notion of the common good, and the desire to protect human beings – or at least, what counts as a human being. Who would disagree with it, in principle? Even Stalin took time out from his savage reconstruction of Russia and the incarceration or murder of so many of its citizens to write a socialist constitution that was based on human rights (Ishay 2004: 211). Thus the problem of human rights is not first of all ideological, but political and representational: everyone agrees with rights (in principle) but cannot (in practice) work out how to protect them in the face of competing and contradictory interests (Alves 2000: 496). As a result, the Universal Declaration and its idea of human rights for all has succeeded marvellously, as ideology. But it has also failed dreadfully: since 1948 there has barely been a moment free from human rights abuses (South Africa, Vietnam, Kampuchea, Palestine, the USA, Chile, Tiananmen Square, Rwanda, Iraq, Afghanistan, Israel, the Lebanon, etc.). Human rights lawyer Costas Douzinas writes:

> The twentieth century is the century of massacre, genocide, ethnic cleansing, the age of the Holocaust. At no point in human history has there been a greater gap between the poor and the rich in the Western world and between the north and south globally. (2000: 2)

The nations of the West are parties to human rights laws, and yet are perfectly capable of excluding from actual material rights – and from the category of Us, those who possess political life by being represented in discourse and in politics – all sorts of particular individuals: the mentally ill, foreigners, convicts, people of colour asylum seekers … the list could go on, indefinitely. And these nations do this while clinging to the mantra of reason, Christian values, attention to balance and order, liberal humanism, and national interests. I do not suggest that these nations or their governments are hypocritical, or only hypocritical. Double standards are inevitable because human rights can only ever be an abstraction. What this means is that it is effectively impossible to be consistent about human rights; and yet the context in which the ideas circulate determine what the discourse can mean for individuals.

MONEY AND RIGHTS

Let me explain this by means of a side trip into the issue of banknotes. While banknotes are, of course, money, they are far more than a mere basis for economic exchange. National currency is not only a system of representation of financial value, but also a system of representation of the nation and its values

(Théret 1999; Tappe 2007). As such, the designs on banknotes are implicated in the nation's attitudes to human being, human good and human rights.

This became something of a media cause following the US invasion of Iraq and the overthrow of Saddam Hussein's regime. At that point, the Iraqi currency carried a portrait of the dictator, and the US authorities considered it a high priority to introduce a new note. Paul Bremer of the Coalition Provisional Authority explained the reasons for this move in an address to the Iraqi people, where as well as the technical implications, he said:

> these bills will not have Saddam's picture on them. You will no longer have to carry the tyrant's portrait with you. ... This new currency is a symbol of the hope in your future. It will be safer and easier for you to use. Beyond that, Saddam is off your money and out of your lives. (2003)

What Bremer's address to the Iraqi people did not point out is that Saddam's image on the banknote served not only as a sign of his control of the nation, but also as a rallying point for Sunni resistance, and a reminder that the USA had not, up to this point, been able to capture Saddam (*IRIN* 2003). Still, it was celebrated in the US media and on blog sites as a human rights gesture, as the symbolic removal of the dictator, as an expression of emancipation for the Iraqi people. No doubt for many Iraqis it was a relief; no doubt for many Americans it was a clear statement of the moral value of invading Iraq.

But once a government so explicitly points out the symbolic impact of images printed on foreign banknotes, it risks drawing attention to its own banknotes and the meanings they make. There is a longstanding complaint within the USA about the representations made by local banknotes, a number of which carry portraits of the Founding Fathers – men who built the nation, yet were also slave owners. One internet company produces shirts, bags, toys and other objects stamped with the slogan STOP PUTTING SLAVE OWNERS ON MONEY, and calls on its customers to 'Help raise awareness with these gifts and apparel' (cafepress, nd). Though the US currency has recently been redesigned, it has not effectively addressed this symbolic impact. One blogger, for instance, in a discussion about the new-look US currency, wrote the laconic comment, 'Still look like baseball cards with slave owners on 'em' (vaxguru 2007).

This may seem a bit unfair; after all, the writers of the Declaration of Independence and the Founding Fathers are by and large on record as being opposed to slavery. In private, at least. Thomas Jefferson, for instance, whose portrait is on the $2 note, is the principal author of the Declaration of Independence and is on record as a very liberal thinker. Indeed, he is something of a poster boy for discussions about the human rights advances offered by the Declaration, but made no moves to emancipate his own slaves. George

Washington, whose portrait is on the $1 note, was also a slave owner who apparently managed his 'property' in a comparatively enlightened manner, but did not free his slaves in his own lifetime. This raises the spectre of the Fathers of Freedom thinking and writing about human rights issues, while consciously ignoring the rights of those human beings listed on their schedules of assets.

This is not to suggest that these historical figures were being disingenuous in their visions of justice and freedom; or that removing Saddam's image from Iraqi banknotes was a pointless act. Those acting as the champions of freedom can also be slave owners because they have been able to reduce both freedom and slavery to abstractions, and thus to forget the concrete materiality of others' existence. What we see in the case of both Iraqi and US currency are layers of representation, existing in layers of history. For Iraq, the banknotes served as a recurrent and inescapable reminder that Saddam was the standard, for local people, of value; that their economic and everyday life depended on and was delimited by him. Removing his portrait was a strong symbolic act, a statement that his power had been vitiated, and his capacity to act as the standard of value had gone. Each version of the Iraqi banknote offers a powerful sign; but who reads it, or is moved by it, is another matter. For instance, I would have great difficulty in saying whose face is on any of the banknotes I use on a daily basis. I pay attention to the dollar value, not the representational sign; and I suspect I am not alone in that. So the Iraqi banknotes bearing Saddam's portrait are both a strong statement, and an easily ignored sign.

But the Founding Fathers' capacity to hold in one body and mind the glorious ideals of the Declaration and their treatment of slaves as commodities, not those 'created equal', not part of the 'all' for whom justice and liberty are promised, is quite another matter. Saddam's face on – and then off – the Iraqi banknotes is a *reminder* of an actuality of inhumanity; the early US system of social organization was the *actualization* of inhumanity. It may be that the images on the US banknotes are, by and large, ignored by their users, but the fact remains that the gap between abstract philosophy and concrete action has barely been plugged; slavery has gone in the USA, driven in no small part by the universalism inherent in the Declaration; but the relations of power and the possibilities of being for many African Americans are a long way from the *Life, Liberty and the Pursuit of Happiness* promised in that Declaration.

The terms and contexts of representation do have significance – representation is, after all, a system of signification. But there is never just one way of framing these terms and contexts, or of reading the outcomes. So, although it seems that the more we proclaim human rights the less we practise them, in fact it would be difficult to do it otherwise given the problem of representation. There is always a lack, a gap between the thing and its articulation. This is particularly marked in human rights discourse because the very thing which is the focus of its attention, humanity, both does and does not refer to individual, concrete instances of *people*.

And this gap has individual, concrete effects. It is not 'humanity' that suffers the lack of human rights, but particular people. It is not 'humanity' that virtually any government would be willing to torment, but particular people. Even in the West, those nations that claim a virtual monopoly over freedom and rights, it is possible to maintain the idea of rights and yet remove particular rights. There have been (too many) instances of just this in recent years, perhaps the most shocking being the incidences of torture carried out by the US soldiers at Abu Ghraib prison. This probably only seems the most shocking because it was shown, again and again, in the news media, and so was forcibly brought to the attention of Western audiences. Nonetheless, it serves as an example of how ordinary, by-and-large democratically-minded people, can represent others as objects of control and force, and not as people. Nor is this behaviour restricted to servants obeying their masters, or young and ill-educated people going beyond their mission: the leaders of Western states have been complicit in reducing people to lumps of flesh that can be tormented in the interests of extracting data. Australian attorney-general Philip Ruddock, for instance, when asked to comment on reported changes to the US military interrogation techniques, complained that 'the US decision to ban torture as an interrogation method outright could make it more difficult to break up terrorist plots' (*Canberra Times* 2006). I am sure it would be difficult for Philip Ruddock to watch a material person – another human – being abused, or deprived of sleep, and still maintain that such practices constitute humane forms of interrogation; but when they are represented as enemy, as object and as idea, it is easy to discount their human being. This is another of the gaps in the story, another Michael K. moment.

TAKING ACTION?

What is the responsibility of any human being, given this context of a gap; the space where, as Certeau writes, 'something needs to be done'? Perhaps what needs to be done is to put representation in its place, and observe it always as *a* way of making sense, not *the* way. Here is where Derrida's notion of representation as undecidability becomes useful. His deconstructionist theory insists on the fact that meaning is never secured; that truth cannot exist in representation because of the effects of *différance* – the slipping between self and other, the deferral of final meaning. This undecidability is the condition of representation, and also marks its limits: it is *something* but not *everything*, because it is never certain, and never completed. The gap is the space where something else might happen. It is an empty space, something that seems to contain or at least refer to the presence of actuality, but contains nothing sure. This could be taken to suggest that nothing can be done, ethically, or even should be done. If anything can mean anything, if there is not certainty or finality, what difference does any political action make? Surely it only becomes more of the emptiness that constitutes human beings and human societies? But for Derrida this thinking leads to an ethics of 'responsibility without autonomy' (Derrida 1995b: 261). We 'ought' to attempt a *something* – to use representation to enact events that can have meaning. Since representation is a matter of making real, of bringing into being, of substituting for, it is also representation that can make real, bring into being and substitute for a more ethical way of living together; not necessarily because it is the 'right' thing to do, but because it is pragmatic. Life is more comfortable when nations and individuals are at peace. The legal frameworks that define our normative roles are open to a range of interpretations, and a practical response would be to interpret them in a way that recognizes the particularity of each person, as a way of raising accord. Even in environmental terms, pragmatism is an ethics, because the planet, the very grounds of our existence, is more capable of supporting us when we care for it.

How to take action is another matter. How does an individual committed to ethical and political action avoid being another Thomas Jefferson – laying down the terms for universal human rights while treating individual humans as commodities? One way is to re-represent: to tell the story from a different point of view. Jeffner Allen states, 'A tale, once heard differently, can be retold' (1989: 45), and many activists do just this: retell a story, reframe it, and use the very principles of representation to fill the gap between abstraction and actuality in a way that suits their interests better. One example can be seen in the work of Palestinian architect and now writer, Suad Amiry. Her work is dedicated to the restoration of traditional Palestinian buildings as a way of showing the long history of their presence in the region, and their very human interaction with the land. She is committed to reworking the representations made of her people in other ways too. Currently, the Western networks tend to show Palestinians in one of two ways. The first is the images of exhausted old men, grieving women and shattered children, living in dire circumstances in refugee camps; the second is furious young men, hurling stones at Israeli soldiers or heading off to become the next wave of suicide bombers. Both are empirically true: certainly these images are not invented. But they are limited and interested images – *limited* in that the entire Palestinian community is framed only as loss or violence, *interested* in that it reinforces the general Western perspective of Arabic people being marked only by lack and otherness. Suad Amiry rejects this:

> Unfortunately, we are always seen as people who are dying, but we want to be seen as people who are living and people who want to live and have a will to continue to live. (Amiry and Brown 2007)

Jeffrey Brown, her interlocutor in this report, points out that Amiry's work is 'about finding ways to normalize life' (2007); that is, it is about working to reframe the story of the Palestinians, and remake their image to the point that the West can see them as part of 'us'. The fact that she is doing this work and telling this story in a way that Western audiences can understand means she is using representation consciously as a means to re-engage the world of lived experience.

The point in this issue is to work consciously with the principles of representation, remembering that however all-encompassing a dominant discourse may seem, it is only that: a discourse. It can only represent people and events from a particular perspective, for a particular reason. Its truth may seem self-evident or beyond discussion, and yet with just a turn of the head, things can be (re)presented differently. People and peoples resisting the forces of domination have, historically, been able to re-present a point of view, or a history, or a logic, and retell the story, showing in the process that it is not a given or natural set of affairs, but a matter of discourse.

V.N. Volosinov explains it thus: 'The domain of ideology coincides with the domain of signs' (1973: 10). This is because representation structures both the relations of power and the relations of idea-to-idea, and idea-to-'truth'. But this does not translate into a process of cutting communities up into small groups who share precisely the same ideology. Rather, everyone in a political or otherwise-constituted group must, as we have seen in earlier chapters, loosely share the basic principles of that community, and certainly share the same sign system – particular linguistic codes, for instance. How they use those codes, however, and how they organize and present signs within those codes, is the site for struggle over the terms of 'truth' and power. 'Various classes will use the same language,' Volosinov goes on to write, and therefore 'differently oriented accents intersect in every ideological sign. Sign becomes the arena of class struggle' (1973: 23).

We have seen in this chapter that struggle is a feature of human society. The gap between how things seem to be, how they are said to be, and how any individual experiences them as being, is a gap in which, very often, something 'should be' done, some political action taken, some theoretical approach worked through. Although representation is constitutive of us, it is still only an artefact of human practice, and therefore able to be put to work by us to get things done. Michel de Certeau urges this, pointing out the limits and the spaces offered by representation:

> Innumerable ways of playing and foiling the other's game, that is, the space instituted by others, characterize the subtle, stubborn, resistant activity of groups which, since they lack their own space, have to get along in a network of already established forces and representations. People have to make do with what they have. (1984: 18)

What we have, by and large, is a dynamic environment that consists of interactions between the abstract, ephemeral logic of representation, and the lived, felt world of experience. It is up to each of us, as subjects of representation and representing subjects, to make sense of the 'already established forces', and play the game in a way that seems to offer, for a moment and a place, the best ethical outcomes.

Glossary

Agency/agents: the term used for any individual or collective that acts in society (noun); also (verb) the work of any individual or collective who acts in society; the capacity to act; see **subject**

Analogy: a phrase or expression that illustrates one idea through the use of another idea or thing that is similar to it; the capacity to identify sameness in difference; often presented in the form of a simile (the sun is like a yellow ball); see **metaphor**

Apartheid (lit., 'apartness'): the doctrine of separate development of people based on racial segregation: developed in South Africa in the mid-twentieth century and cause of immense suffering and deprivation for the African peoples of that nation

Axiology/axiological: a branch of philosophy that focuses on the study of value, including ethics

Bare life: term used by the Italian philosopher Giorgio Agamben; refers to *zoë*, or 'the mere state of being alive', as distinct from political life which incorporates rights and protections; those who possess only bare life are exposed, like the sacrificial offerings of ancient religions, to political violence and death without any rights of appeal or redress; see **subject**

Binary oppositions: the basic organizational structure of much of western society, which sets two related objects or concepts in a paired, oppositional relationship; one of the pair is always dominant over the other; see *différance*

Bullshit: a type of misrepresentation; a term used by philosopher Harry Frankfurt to explain the process by which **agents** (social actors) obscure the actual state of things; having no concern for the truth

Chora: the prelingual state of the infant; term used by Julia Kristeva, Jacques Derrida and others to describe the state of being halfway between complete unknowing (the foetus) and the capacity to take a place in the **symbolic order**

Cogito (Latin, 'I think'): the term used by Rene Descartes to express his understanding of human being as located in the capacity to think (short form of *'cogito, ergo sum'*; or, 'I think, therefore I am')

Cognition/cognitive: the processes of the brain that organize and arrange knowledge; related to thought, reason and creativity

Constative utterance: the linguistic term, used by J.L. Austin, for propositional statements – statements about the world that describe a state of affairs; see **performative utterance**

Cultural industries: those industries involved in generating and developing intellectual property, including film, art, design, creative writing, IT and digital products; also known as the creative or consciousness industries

Différance: Jacques Derrida's term that encompasses both the *difference* that is the basis of the **symbolic order,** and the *deferral* that is always part of any communication because final or perfect meaning can never be attained

Discourse: ways of constructing and organizing knowledge that pertain to a particular social or cultural field; the forms of language that are both associated with, and express the values of, those fields; see **episteme**

Enlightenment, the: the beginning of the modern age; characterized by a massive outpouring of philosophical thought and political actions, and by a shift from tradition and mysticism to reason, and from divine law to human law

Episteme: term associated with Michel Foucault for periods of history that organized around and in terms of specific worldviews and **discourses**

Epistemology/epistemological: the branch of philosophy that is concerned with theories of knowledge: how we know the things we know

Habitus: a term associated with Pierre Bourdieu, and used to describe 'second nature' – an individual's mostly unconscious dispositions, learned behaviours, and tendencies; it expresses how individuals 'become themselves', and how they engage in practices

Icon: a term associated with C.S. Pierce for a sign that is a direct representation of something already known, or a simulacrum for something in the real world; e.g., a photograph that looks like its subject; see **index, referent, sign, symbol**

Ideology/ideological: the matrix that frames what we can see, and what we can imagine; the practice whereby a particular group within a culture attempts to naturalize their own meanings and values, or pass them off as universal and as common sense

Imagined communities: a phrase associated with Benedict Anderson, to explain the ways in which nations and other communities, made up of many disparate individuals, come to seem real, necessary and natural collections of people who belong together through the effects of the mass media, stories of origin, and traditions

Index: a term associated with C.S. Pierce for a sign that does not resemble its referent, but is influenced and acted upon by it; e.g., a weather vane that signals the direction of the wind by being acted on the wind; see **icon, referent, sign, symbol**

Interpellate/interpellation: the term associated with Louis Althusser that explains how people become **subjects** through being named as such by authorities – inter [within] and appellation [the act of naming]

Leviathan: Thomas Hobbes' metaphor for the state, and for the relations of, and struggle for, power between citizens and state

Logocentric: an analytical method that pays excessive attention to spoken and written language, to the exclusion of other forms of communication and representation; a way of thinking that assumes and relies on an external reality and a unitary truth that can be discovered, or uncovered, by the use of scientific method and reason; see **metaphysics of presence**

Master signifier: a term associated with the work of Jacques Lacan; the **sign**, or **signifier**, that itself has no **signified** (i.e., an empty signifier), but is the basis of meaning-making for all other signs in a particular discourse, that provides them with a point of reference and a point of anchor for their own meanings

Metaphor: a figure of speech in which a word or phrase literally signifying one object or idea is applied to another; a substitutionary representation, in which the primary object is transformed into something else, suggesting a likeness or analogy between them; e.g., 'the road was a ribbon across the field'; see **analogy**

Metaphysics of presence: the concept that behind all our representations is a concrete reality; that the terms we use to describe things are connected to actual ideas or objects, from which the terms draw their meaning; see **logocentric**

Mimesis: resemblance; central to ancient Greek thought on representation; understood as the representation of reality, of showing in a text the actual state of things; see **metaphysics of presence**; see **resemblance**

Mirror notion: a term drawn from political theory; the idea that parliamentary representatives should mirror the population as a whole, with proportional representation of all the groups and interests found in that population

Mirror phase: drawn from the work of Jacques Lacan; this is the point at which an infant first realizes they are separate from the rest of the world; the constitutive point of identity predicated on separation

Ontology/ontological: the branch of philosophy that focuses on theories of being, or existence

Performative utterance: a linguistic term associated with J.L. Austin for utterances that perform, or are part of the performance, of an action; have no concern with truth or falsehood or with description, only with doing; see **constative utterance**

Phenomenology/phenomenological: the branch of philosophy that focuses on experience, and the objectivities associated with experiences

Qualia: a term drawn from the philosophy of mind; the feeling of being and of various states and experiences; the phenomenological aspects of life

Referent: the concrete object or idea that is named – referred to, or designated – by a word or expression; that which is referred to by a sign and which, through a process of establishing equivalences between referent and sign, secures meaning; see **signified**; see **sign**

Resemblance: the form of communication or signification in which a sign, in some degree, resembles its referent; see **mimesis**; see **simulacrum**

Semiotics: the 'science' or study of signs; an approach to language that deals with how words and signs make meanings; the notion that all communication is based on signs – things that stand for other things

Signifier: the representative element of a sign; the word, image or sound used to refer to something; see **signified**; see **sign**

Signified: the represented element of a sign; the concrete object or idea that gives a signifier its content; see **metaphysics of presence**; see **referent**; see **signifier**

Sign: something that stands in for, or represents, an absent object, idea or person; for Ferdinand de Saussure, is the combination of the signifier and the signified; for C.S. Peirce, is 'something which stands to somebody for something'

Simulacrum: a resemblance that is taken to perfectly duplicate the original; for Jean Baudrillard, is not a likeness, but a reality in its own right: the hyperreal; see **resemblance**

Social contract: social theory dating from **the Enlightenment** that examines human beings in communities; the implied agreement by which individuals agree to give up certain freedoms for the good of the community; the basis for civil society and representative democracy; see **Leviathan**

Subjects: individuals who possess social existence; members of the social and **symbolic order**; see **bare life**; see **agent**

Symbol: a term associated with C.S. Pierce for a sign that has no necessary connection with its referent; a symbol is understood only because there are shared conventional meanings for it; see **icon, index, referent, sign**

Symbolic order: the domain of all social existence, a linguistic domain; predicated on difference – between self and other, subject and object – and on the capacity to take up a place as a social subject

Symbolic power: power grounded on representation; the capacity to bring things into objective existence through the symbolic properties of language to name those things and make them explicit

Ubuntu: the doctrine that comes from sub-Saharan Africa, and focuses on the allegiances and responsibilities all people have towards all others; often expressed as 'A person is only a person in relation to other persons'

References

ABC (Australian Broadcasting Corporation) (2007) 'The Seven O'Clock News' (headline), 27 March.

Abish, Walter (1974) *Alphabetical Africa,* New York: New Directions Books.

Adorno, Theodor (1981) *Prisms* (trans Samuel and Shierry Weber), Cambridge, MA: MIT Press.

Adorno, Theodor (1991) *The culture industry: selected essays on mass culture* (edited with an introduction by J. M. Bernstein), London: Routledge.

Agamben, Giorgio (1998) *Homo sacer: sovereign power and bare life* (trans Daniel Heller-Roazen), Stanford: Stanford University Press.

Allen, Jeffner (1989) 'Women who beget women must thwart major sophisms', in Ann Garry and Marilyn Pearsall (eds), *Women, knowledge and reality: explorations in feminist philosophy,* Winchester: Unwin Hymen, 37–46.

Althusser, Louis (1994) 'Ideology and state ideological apparatuses (notes towards an investigation)', in Slavoj Zizek (ed.), *Mapping ideology,* London and New York: Verso, 100–40.

Alves, José A Lindgren (2000) 'The Declaration of Human Rights in postmodernity', *Human Rights Quarterly* 22, 478–500.

Amiry, Suad and Jeffrey Brown (2007) 'Mideast architect turns to words', *Jim Lehrer NewsHour,* PBS Television, 3 April.

Anderson, Benedict (1983) *Imagined communities: reflections on the origin and spread of nationalism,* London and New York: Verso.

Ankersmit, Frank (2003) 'Pygmalion: Rousseau and Diderot on the theatre and on representation', *Rethinking History* 7 (3): 315–39.

Arendt, Hannah (1966) *The origins of totalitarianism,* New York: Harcourt Brace Jovanovich.

Atwood, Margaret (1983) 'This is a photograph of me', in A. Allison, H. Barrows, C. R. Blake, A. J. Carr, A. E. Eastman and H. M. English (eds), *The Norton Anthology of Poetry* (third edn), London and New York: Norton, 1373–4.

Austin, J. L. (1975) *How to do things with words* (second edn), Cambridge: Harvard University Press.

Bakhtin, M. M. (1981) *The dialogic imagination* (trans Caryl Emerson and Michael Holquist), Austin: University of Texas Press.

Baron-Cohen, Simon (1995) *Mindblindness: an essay on autism and theory of mind,* Cambridge, MA: MIT Press.

Barthes, Roland (1981) *Camera lucida: reflections on photography* (trans Richard Howard), New York: Hill & Wang.

Barthes, Roland (1985) *The responsibility of forms: critical essays on music, art, and representation* (trans Richard Howard), New York: Hill & Wang.

Baudrillard, Jean (1983) *Simulations* (trans Paul Foss, Paul Patton and Philip Beitchman), New York: Semiotext(e).

Baudrillard, Jean (2001) *Selected writings* (edited and introduced by Mark Poster), Cambridge: Polity.

Baudrillard, Jean (2002) *The spirit of terrorism and requiem for the Twin Towers* (trans Chris Turner), London and New York: Verso.

Beckett, Samuel (1964) *Play*, London: Faber & Faber.

Belsey, Catherine (1980) *Critical practice*, London: Routledge.

Benveniste, Emile (1971) *Problems in general linguistics* (trans Mary Elizabeth Meek), Coral Gables: University of Miami Press.

Bergson, Henri (1946) *The creative mind* (trans Mabelle L. Andison), New York: The Wisdom Library.

Bhabha, Homi (1983) 'The other question ... Homi Bhabha reconsiders the stereotype and colonial discourse', *Screen Incorporating Screen Education* 23 (6): Nov–Dec, 18–36.

Birch, A. H. (1971) *Representation*, London: Pall Mall Press.

Boss, Shira (2007) 'Even in a virtual world, "stuff" matters', *New York Times* electronic version, 9 September, http://www.nytimes.com/2007/09/09/business/yourmoney/09second.html?_r=2&ref=yourmoney&oref=slogin&oref=slogin (accessed 13 September 2007)

Bourdieu, Pierre (1975) 'The specificity of the scientific field and the social conditions of the progress of reason', *Social Science Information* 14 (6): 19–47.

Bourdieu, Pierre (1977) *Outline of a theory of practice* (trans Richard Nice), Cambridge: Cambridge University Press.

Bourdieu, Pierre (1987) 'What makes a social class? On the theoretical and practical existence of groups' (trans Loic Wacquant and David Young), *Berkeley Journal of Sociology* 1–17.

Bourdieu, Pierre (1991) *Language and symbolic power* (ed. John B. Thompson, trans Gino Raymond and Matthew Adamson), Cambridge: Polity.

Bowles, Kate (2002) 'Representation', in Stuart Cunningham and Graeme Turner (eds), *The media and communications in Australia*, Sydney: Allen and Unwin, 72–84.

Boyle, Danny (2007), in interview with Margaret Polanz, *The Movie Show*, SBS Television, 4 April.

Bremer, L. Paul (2003) 'Address to the Iraqi People', the Coalition Provisional Authority, 10 September, http://www.cpa-iraq.org/transcripts/20031011_Oct 10bremerbroadcast.htm (accessed 27 September 2005).

Buchloh, Benjamin H. D. (1984) 'Figures of authority, ciphers of regression: notes on the return of representation in European painting', in Brian Wallis (ed.), *Art after modernism: rethinking representation*, The New Museum of Contemporary Art, New York in association with David R. Godine Publisher, Boston, 107–35.

Butler, Judith (1990) *Gender trouble: feminism and the subversion of identity*, New York: Routledge.

Buzzetti, Dino (2002) 'Digital representation and the text model', *New Literary History* 33 (1): 61–88.

cafepress, catalogue, http://www.cafepress.com/bytelandart/544428 (accessed 7 November 2007).

Canberra Times (2006) 'Sleep deprivations "humane"', 2 October, 1.

Carter, Paul (2004) *Material thinking: the theory and practice of creative research*, Carlton: Melbourne University Publishing.

Certeau, Michel de (1984) *The practice of everyday life* (trans Steven Rendall), Berkeley: University of California Press.

Certeau, Michel de (1986) *Heterologies: discourse on the other* (trans Brian Massumi), Minneapolis: University of Minnesota Press.

Chartier, Roger (1997) *On the edge of the cliff: history, language, and practice* (trans Lydia Cochrane), Baltimore and London: Johns Hopkins University Press.

Coetzee, J. M. (1983) *The life and times of Michael K*, Harmondsworth: Penguin.

Colebrook, Claire (2000) 'Questioning representation', *SubStance*, 29 (2): 47–67.

Collis, Paul (2007) Personal communication, Canberra, 5 March.

Crane Tim (2002) 'Intentional objects', in Emma Borg (ed.), *Meaning and representation*, Oxford: Blackwell, 43–57.

Critchley, Simon (2004) *Very little … almost nothing: death, philosophy, literature* (second edn), London and New York: Routledge.

Critchley, Simon (2005) *Things merely are*, London and New York: Routledge.

Cummings, E. E. (1983 [1923]) 'r-p-o-p-h-e-s-s-a-g-r', in A. Allison, H. Barrows, C. R. Blake, A. J. Carr, A. E. Eastman and H. M. English (eds), *The Norton Anthology of Poetry* (third edn), London and New York: Norton, 1044.

Cunningham, Stuart (1997) 'Television', in Stuart Cunningham and Graeme Turner (eds), *The Media in Australia: industries, texts, audiences* (second edn) St. Leonards: Allen & Unwin, 90–111.

Cunningham, Stuart and Graeme Turner (eds) (1997) *The Media in Australia: industries, texts, audiences* (second edn), St Leonards: Allen & Unwin.

Damasio, Antonio (1995) *Descartes' error: emotion, reason and the human brain*, New York: Quill.

Damasio, Antonio (2000) *The feeling of what happens: body, emotion and the making of consciousness,* London: Vintage.

Debord, Guy (1977) *The society of the spectacle,* Detroit: Black & Red.

Deleuze, Gilles (1972) 'Intellectuals and power' (in conversation with Michel Foucault), in M. Foucault (1977) *Language, counter-memory, practice: selected essays and interviews* (trans Donald F. Bouchard and Sherry Simon), Ithaca, NY: Cornell University Press, 205–17.

Deleuze, Gilles (1990) *The logic of sense* (trans Mark Lester with Charles Stivale), New York: Columbia University Press.

Deleuze, Gilles (1991) *Empiricism and subjectivity: an essay on Hume's theory of human nature* (trans Constantin V. Boundas), New York: Columbia.

Deleuze, Gilles (1994) *Difference and repetition* (trans Paul Patton), London: Athlone.

Dennett, Daniel (1991) *Consciousness explained*, Harmondsworth: Penguin.

Dennett, Daniel (1995) *Darwin's dangerous idea: evolution and the meanings of life*, New York: Simon & Schuster.

Derrida, Jacques (1968) 'Différance,' in J. Derrida (1982) *Margins of philosophy* (trans Alan Bass), Brighton: Harvester Press, 1–27.

Derrida, Jacques (1974) *Of grammatology* (trans Gayatri Spivak), Baltimore, MD: Johns Hopkins University Press.

Derrida, Jacques (1982) 'Sending: on representation' (trans P. Caws and M. A. Caws), *Social Research*, Summer, 294–326

Derrida, Jacques (1995a) *On the name* (ed. T. Dutoit), Stanford: Stanford University Press.

Derrida, Jacques (1995b) *Points ...: Interviews, 1974–1994* (ed. Elisabeth Weber, trans Peggy Kamuf et al.), Stanford, CA: Stanford University Press.

Derrida, Jacques (2003) 'Autoimmunity: real and symbolic suicides: a dialogue with Jacques Derrida' (trans Pascale-Anne Brault and Michael Nass), in Giovanna Borradori (ed.), *Philosophy in a time of terror: dialogues with Jurgen Habermas and Jacques Derrida*, Chicago and London: University of Chicago Press, 85–136.

Descartes, René (1969) *The philosophical works of Descartes* (trans E. S. Haldane and G. R. T. Ross), Cambridge: Cambridge University Press.

Dickerson, A. B. (2004) *Kant on representation and objectivity*, Cambridge: Cambridge University Press.

Diprose, Rosalyn (1991) 'A "genethics" that makes sense', in Rosalyn Diprose and Robyn Ferrell (eds), *Cartographies: poststructuralism and the mapping of bodies*, North Sydney: Allen & Unwin, 65–76.

Douzinas, Costas (2000) *The end of human rights: critical legal thought at the turn of the century*, Oxford and Portland, Oregon: Hart Publishing.

Durkheim, Emile (1965) *The elementary forms of the religious life* (trans Joseph Ward Swain), New York: Free Press.

Eco, Umberto (1986a) *Art and beauty in the Middle Ages* (trans Hugh Bredin), New Haven and London: Yale University Press.

Eco, Umberto (1986b) *Travels in hyperreality* (trans William Weaver), London: Picador.

Eliot, T. S. (1969) *The complete poems and plays of T.S. Eliot*, London: Faber and Faber.

Foucault, Michel (1970) *The order of things* (trans Alan Sheridan), New York: Pantheon.

Foucault, Michel (1980) *Power/knowledge,* Harvester: Brighton.

Foucault, Michel (1983) *This is not a pipe* (trans James Harkness), Berkeley: University of California Press.

Fox, Douglas (2004) 'Do fruit flies dream of electric bananas?', in *New Scientist*, 14 February, 32–5.

Frankfurt, Harry G. (2005) *On bullshit*, Princeton and Oxford: Princeton University Press.

Graham, W. S. (1975) 'What is the language using us for?' *Poetry Nation*, 4, 40–44.

Gregg, John (2002) 'Cognition as opposed to qualia' at http://home.comcast.net/~johnrgregg/cognitio.htm (accessed 17 July 2005).

Grosz, Elizabeth (2005) 'Bergson, Deleuze and Becoming'; seminar presentation, University of Queensland, http://www.ched.uq.edu.au/ElizabethGroszpaper1.rtf (accessed 13 July 2006)

Hall, Stuart (1977) 'Culture, the media and the ideological effect', in J. Curran et al. (eds), *Mass communication and society*, London: Edward Arnold.

Hall, Stuart (1997a) 'The work of representation', in S. Hall (ed.), *Representation: cultural representation and signifying practices*, London: Sage in association with Open University Press, 15–74.

Hall, Stuart (1997b) 'Introduction', in S. Hall (ed.) *Representation: cultural representation and signifying practices*, London: Sage in association with Open University Press, 1–11.

Heidegger, Martin (1949) 'Existence and being', in Walter Kaufman (ed.), *Existentialism from Dostoyevsky to Sartre*, http://www.marxists.org/reference/subject/philosophy/works/ge/heidegg2.htm (accessed 2 February 2006)

Hertzberg, Hendrik (2006) 'The talk of the town: the Iraq Report', *New Yorker* December 18, 3–34.

Hirshfield, Jane (1997) *Nine gates: entering the mind of poetry*, New York: HarperCollins.

Hobbes, Thomas (1947 [1651]) *Leviathan* (ed. Michael Oakeshott), Oxford: Basil Blackwell.

Ignatieff, Michael (1994) *Blood and belonging: journeys into the new nationalism*, New York: Farrar, Straus & Giroux.

IRIN (2003) 'New currency on the way', Report, 6 October http://www.iqdclub.com/pages/3/ (accessed 27 September 2005)

Ishay, Micheline (2004) *The history of human rights*, Berkeley: University of California Press.

Izzard, Eddie (1998) *Dress to kill* (DVD), Larry Jordan (dir.), Roadshow Entertainment.

James, William (1967) *The writings of William James*, New York: Random House.

Jay, Martin (1993) *Downcast eyes: on the denigration of vision in twentieth-century French thought*, Berkeley, Los Angeles and London: University of California Press.

Johnson, Mark (1987) *The body in the mind: the bodily basis of meaning, imagination, and reason*, Chicago: University of Chicago Press.

Judovitz, Dalia (1988) *Subjectivity and representation in Descartes: the origins of modernity*, Cambridge: Cambridge University Press.

Kant, Immanuel (1987) *Critique of judgment* (trans Werner S. Pluhar), Indianapolis: Hackett.

Kress, Gunther and Theo van Leeuwen (1996) *Reading images: the grammar of visual design*, London and New York: Routledge.

Lacan, Jacques (1977a) *The four fundamental concepts of psycho-analysis* (trans Alan Sheridan), Harmondsworth: Penguin.

Lacan, Jacques (1977b) *Ecrits: a selection* (trans Alan Sheridan), London: Tavistock/Routledge.

Laclau, Ernesto (1988) 'Metaphor and social antagonism', in C. Nelson and L. Grossberg (eds) *Marxism and the interpretation of culture,* Urbana: University of Illinois Press, 249–57.

Laclau, Ernesto (1990) *New reflections on the revolution of our time*, London: Verso.

Laclau, Ernesto and Chantal Mouffe (1985) *Hegemony and socialist strategy: towards a radical democratic politics,* London and New York: Verso.

Lakoff, George and Mark Johnson (1980) *Metaphors we live by*, Chicago: University of Chicago Press.

Lefort, Claude (1986) *The political forms of modern society: bureaucracy, democracy, totalitarianism* (ed. John B Thompson), Cambridge, MA: MIT Press.

Lefort, Claude (1988) *Democracy and political theory* (trans David Macey), Minneapolis: University of Minnesota Press.

Levi, Primo (2007 [1978]) 'A tranquil star' (trans Ann Goldstein), *The New Yorker* 12 February, 72– 4.

Locke, John (1975 [1690]) *An essay concerning human understanding* (ed. Peter H Nidditch), Oxford: Oxford University Press.

Los Angeles Times (2007) 'Men and women in doubt about new sex symbols', *Sydney Morning Herald*, 'World' section, January, 13–14.

Lovelace, Richard (1983 [1649]) 'The grasshopper', in A. Allison, H. Barrows, C.R. Blake, A. J. Carr, A. E. Eastman and H. M. English (eds), *The Norton Anthology of Poetry* (third edn), London and New York: Norton, 334.

Marin, Louis (2001) *On representation* (trans Catherine Porter), Stanford, CA: Stanford University Press.

Marx, Karl and Engels, Frederick (1976 [c.1845]) *The German Ideology*, Moscow: Progress Publishers.

Maturana, Humberto and Francisco Varela (1980) *Autopoiesis and cognition: the realization of the living*, Dordrecht: D Reidel.

Merleau-Ponty, Maurice (1962) *Phenomenology of perception* (trans Colin Smith), London: Routledge.

Merleau-Ponty, Maurice (1964) *Sense and non-sense* (trans Hubert L. Dreyfus and Patricia Allen Dreyfus), Evanston: Northwestern University Press.

Merleau-Ponty, Maurice (1968) *The visible and the invisible* (ed. Claude Lefort, trans Alfonso Lingis), Evanston: Northwestern University Press.

Mill, John Stuart (1975 [1861]) *Three essays*, Oxford: Oxford University Press.

Montaigne, Michel de (1987) *Four essays* (trans M. A. Screech), London and New York: Penguin.

Mzamane, Mbulelo (2001) Personal communication, Australian National University, Canberra, 1 June.

Nancy, Jean-Luc (1993) 'The sublime offering', in Jean-Francois Courtine (ed.), *Of the sublime: presence in question* (trans Jeffrey S Librett), Albany: SUNY UP, 25–53.

Nietzsche, Friedrich (1967) *The birth of tragedy and the case of Wagner* (trans Walter Kaufmann), New York: Vintage.

Nietzsche, Friedrich (1968) *The will to power* (trans W. Kaufmann and R.J. Hollingdale), New York: Vintage Books.

O'Sullivan, Tim, John Hartley, Danny Saunders, Martin Montgomery and John Fiske (1994) *Key concepts in communication and cultural studies*, London: Routledge.

Østergård, Svend (1996) 'The unconscious of representation ("Death and the Compass")' *Variaciones Borges* 1, 101–12.

Paine, Thomas (1969) *Rights of man* (ed. Henry Collins), Harmondsworth: Penguin.

Pateman, Carole (1985) *The problem of political obligation: a critique of liberal theory*, Cambridge: Polity.

Peirce, Charles Sanders (1955) *Philosophical writings of Peirce* (edited and with an introduction by Justus Buchler), Dover Publications, New York.

Prendergast, Christopher (2000) *The triangle of representation,* New York: Columbia University Press.

Rauch, Angelica (1996) 'Saving philosophy in cultural studies: the case of mother wit', *PMC: Postmodern Culture, an electronic journal of interdisciplinary criticism* 7.1, September, http://www3.iath.virginia.edu/pmc/text-only/issue.996/rauch.996 (accessed 17 July 2005)

Rauth, Eric (2002) 'The blasphemer's *Art De Faire'*, *Cultural Critique* 52, Fall, 10–39.

Rorty, Richard (1980) *Philosophy and the mirror of nature*, Oxford: Blackwell.

Rousseau, Jean-Jacques (1968 [1762]) *The social contract* (trans Maurice Cranston), Harmondsworth: Penguin.

Said, Edward W. (1978) *Orientalism*, Harmondsworth: Penguin.

Saussure, Ferdinand de (1966) *Course in general linguistics* (trans Wade Baskin), New York: McGraw-Hill.

Sawer, Marion, and Gianni Zappalà (eds) (2001) *Speaking for the people: representation in Australian politics*, Carlton South: Penguin.

Scarry, Elaine (1985)*The body in pain: the making and unmaking of the world*, New York and Oxford: Oxford University Press.

Schopenhauer, Arthur (1969) *The world as will and representation* (trans E.F.J. Payne), New York: Dover.

Schwartz, Nancy L. (1988) *The blue guitar: political representation and community*, Chicago: University of Chicago Press.

Searle, John R. (1993) 'Metaphor' in Andrew Ortony (ed.), *Metaphor and thought* (second edn), Cambridge: Cambridge University Press, 83–111.

Slaughter, Joseph (1997) 'A question of narration: the voice in international human rights law', *Human Rights Quarterly* 19 (2): 406–30.

Stafford, Barbara (1999) *Visual analogy: consciousness as the art of connecting*, Cambridge, MA and London: MIT Press.

Tappe, Oliver (2007) 'A new banknote in the People's Republic. The iconography of the Kip and ideological transformations in Laos, 1957–2006', *Internationales Asienforum* 38: 1–2, 87–108.

Théret, Bruno (1999) 'The socio-political dimensions of the currency: implications for the transition to the Euro', *Journal of Consumer Policy* 22: 51–79.

Thomassen, Lasse (2006) 'Beyond representation?', *Parliamentary Affairs* http://pa .oxfordjournals.org/cgi/content/full/gsl051v1#RFN3 (accessed 3 January 2007)

Tschaepe, M. D. (2003) 'Halo of identity: the significance of first names and naming' *Janus Head* 6: 67–78.

Tsur, Reuven (2002) 'Aspects of cognitive poetics', in Elena Semino and Jonathan Culpeper (eds), *Cognitive stylistics – language and cognition in text analysis*, Amsterdam and Philadelphia: John Benjamins Publishing Company.

Turner, Graeme (1997) 'Media texts and messages', in Stuart Cunningham and Graeme Turner (eds), *The Media in Australia: industries, texts, audiences* (second edn), St. Leonards: Allen & Unwin, 90–111.

Updike, John (1989) *Self-consciousness*, New York: Alfred A Knopf.

van Oort, Richard (2003) 'Cognitive science and the problem of representation', *Poetics Today* 24 (2): 237–95.

vaxguru (2007) http://digg.com/business_finance/The_New_Colors_of_U_S_ Money, 22 September (accessed 25 September 2007)

Virilio, Paul (2000) *The information bomb* (trans Chris Turner), London and New York: Verso.

Volosinov, V. N. (1973 [1930]) *Marxism and the philosophy of language* (trans Ladislav Matejka and I. R. Titunik), New York: Seminar.

Whately, Alice (2000) *Contemporary Eastern: interiors from the Orient*, Frenchs Forest, Australia: Holland Publishers.

Wittgenstein, Ludwig (1922) *Tractatus Logico-Philosophicus* (trans C. K. Ogden, introduction by Bertrand Russell), London: Routledge.

Wittgenstein, Ludwig (1958) *Philosophical investigations* (third edn; trans G.E.M. Anscombe), New York: Macmillan.

Zizek, Slavoj (1991) *Looking awry: an introduction to Jacques Lacan through popular culture*, Cambridge, MA: MIT Press.

Zizek, Slavoj (1994) 'Introduction: the spectre of ideology', in S. Zizek (ed.), *Mapping ideology*, London and New York: Verso, 1–33.

Index

Glossary definitions are indicated by 'def' before the page number